1/14/13
$23.00

Freud

Freud

Jacques Sédat

Translated by
Susan Fairfield

OTHER
Other Press
New York

This book was originally published in France by Editions Armand Colin as *Freud*, copyright © 2000.

Translation copyright © 2005 Susan Fairfield

Production Editor: Mira S. Park

This book was set in 11 pt. Berkeley by Alpha Graphics of Pittsfield, NH.

10 9 8 7 6 5 4 3 2 1

Library of Congress Cataloging-in-Publication Data

Sédat, Jacques.
[Freud. English]
Freud / by Jacques Sédat ; translated by Susan Fairfield.
   p. cm.
Includes bibliographical references and index.
ISBN 1-59051-006-2 (pbk. : alk. paper) 1. Freud, Sigmund, 1856–1939.
2. Psychoanalysts—Austria—Biography. I. Title.
BF109.F74S42 2005
150.19'52'092—dc22
                        2005000181

Contents

Part III. The Meaning of Freudianism

Part I

Method

1

Freud's Writing

Sigmund Freud is the author of a considerable body of work: seventeen volumes in German, twenty-three in English, and twenty-one in the French edition now in progress. And this does not include a substantial correspondence: more than 4,000 letters have been preserved, of which 3,200 have been published, letters dealing directly with his thought, theoretical orientations, clinical advice to his students, editorial undertakings, and a politics of psychoanalysis. Freud combined several activities: psychoanalytic practice (for many years ten patients a day, each seen for fifty-five minutes), scientific meetings and conferences (he was a brilliant extempore speaker), the writing of his books, papers, and handwritten correspondence (until late into the night), and the organization of the International Psychoanalytic Association (the IPA, which went from three national associations in 1908 to about twenty in 1938).

THE BIRTH OF PSYCHOANALYSIS

The scope of this volume is limited to a study of Freud's psychoanalytic work and does not discuss his task as founder of a new discipline, psychoanalysis, meant to be regulated by institutions ensuring the training and authorization of psychoanalysts. Freud was originally a neurologist, and he came to psychoanalysis from this standpoint. At the end of the case of Elisabeth von R. in *Studies on Hysteria* (Breuer and Freud 1893–1895), he explains:

> I have not always been a psychotherapist. Like other neuropathologists, I was trained to employ local diagnoses and electro-prognosis, and it still strikes me as strange that the case histories [*Krankengeschichten*]* I write should read like short stories [*Novellen*] and that, as one might say, they lack the serious stamp of science [*Wissenschaftlichkeit*]. I must console myself with the reflection that the nature of the subject is evidently responsible for this, rather than any preference of my own. The fact is that local diagnosis and electrical reactions lead nowhere in the study of hysteria, whereas a detailed description [*Darstellung*] of mental processes [*seelischen Vorgänge*] such as we are accustomed to find in the works of imaginative writers [*Dichter*] enables me, after the use of a few psychological formulas, to obtain at least some kind of insight into the cause of that affection. Case histories [*Krankengeschichten*] of this kind are intended to be judged like psychiatric ones; they have, however, one advantage over the latter, namely an intimate connection between the story of the patient's sufferings [*Leidensgeschichten*] and the symptoms of his illness— a connection for which we search in vain in the biographies of other psychoses. [pp. 160–161]

---

*Translator's note: the German words from Freud's original texts are supplied by the author.

This text is, first of all, concerned to put the "scientificity" of psychoanalysis into perspective and to bring the literary genre of case histories closer to the "stories" bound up with a person's unique history. But its main purpose is to contrast a case history, which is analytic, with a history of the symptom, which is psychiatric: on the one hand, symptoms are seen as related to the subject's history, to his suffering and his subjective experience; on the other, the patient is merely the support for a certain number of signs that the psychiatrist catalogs independently of the subject's suffering and especially of the psychic processes at work in symptom formation.

It is precisely this concept of psychic processes that, for Freud, does away with the antithesis maintained elsewhere between theory and practice. For in psychoanalytic treatment what analysand and analyst have in common are psychic processes, the psychic activity of both parties. Whereas the psychiatric situation revolves around the physician, who establishes the illness on the basis of his gaze, which inventories and organizes signs, the analytic situation is centered on the transferential relationship that brings about a new scene in which the analysand can refuse to accept his story, his subjective past.

LITERARY GENRES

Thus, for Freud, there are no texts setting forth as separate matters a practical view and a theoretical view, but only texts that, from various perspectives, privilege psychic activity. In addition to those of Freud's works that undertake to tell patients' stories, there are two other literary genres: metapsychological texts and texts devoted to technical recommendations. Freud (1915a) is careful to define his metapsychological treatises: "I propose that when we have succeeded in describing a psychical process [the same term used in 1893–1895] in its dynamic, topographical and economic aspects, we should speak of it as a *metapsychological* presentation. We must say at once that in the present state of our knowledge there are only a few points at which we shall succeed in this" (p. 181; emphasis in original).

The papers involving technical recommendations or information about method, papers in which we again find the expression *psychic activity*, are all aimed at helping the analyst find the position from which the patient's transference can be sustained and analyzed at the same time. They all come down to warning the analyst against an attitude of suggestion, mastery, or superior knowledge analogous to that of the psychiatrist, recommending that he adopt an "evenly suspended attention" toward the patient's psychic activity, that is, as needs be, moving from one psychic position to another (1912b, p. 111).

THE PRIMARY IMPORTANCE OF PSYCHIC PROCESSES

The literary genres in which Freud writes psychoanalysis—case histories, metapsychological writings, and technical advice for analyst and analysand—all stress the primary importance of the analyst's and patient's psychic processes. Even the writings on culture (*Totem and Taboo* [1913a], *Civilisation and Its Discontents* [1930], *Moses and Monotheism* [1939a]) are intended to transform mythology into the conditions necessary for the construction of a subject and the impact of cultural factors—the prohibition of incest and the rules governing marriage, religion, law, and political organization—in the process of subject formation. Yet Freud maintains that the discipline he is founding is not based on a world view or a proposal for a new cultural model. In a paper addressed to scientists, "The Claims of Psycho-Analysis to Scientific Interest" [1913c], he places psychoanalysis among the natural sciences (*Naturwissenschaften*), not among the humanities (*Geisteswissenschaften*), because psychoanalysis, like all scientific disciplines, proceeds by example, evolves through new discoveries, and is closest to clinical observation.

PSYCHOANALYSIS AND SCIENCE

Psychoanalysis is not a speculative theory but a scientific approach based on empirical interpretation (1914a). For Freud, this relativization of theory and the theoretical is based on an analysis of the drive for knowledge (*Wisstrieb*) in the child. This is not an original drive but is dependent on another factor, the drive for mastery, an initial mode of gaining knowledge that consists in breaking or devouring the world in order to understand it (the child brings everything to his mouth). Thus the origin of the theory for the child is coextensive with his own psychic processes. Children's sexual theories (cf. 1908a) are their first way of responding to the vitally urgent and narcissistically invested question: Where do children come from?, a question that also bears on the origin and difference of the sexes. These theories, three in number, are the partial answers the child comes up with in his solitary investigations: the theory of the woman with a penis or hermaphroditic theory, denying sexual difference; the cloacal theory of birth in ignorance of the vaginal cavity of the female body; and the sadistic theory of coitus with the division into strong and weak in place of the division into man and woman. These partial theories accompany the elaboration of the body image and determine the capacity for intellectual investigation or intellectual inhibition. The close connection that Freud establishes between the subject's body image and his investigation reminds us that delusion, as viewed by psychoanalysis, is merely an attempt at the self-cure of a flaw in the body image, an attempt that, like children's sexual theories, contains a bit of truth.

In this account of Freud's work I am following the chronological order of his discoveries, his first tentative efforts, and his theoretical revisions made in the light of clinical innovations. This is the procedure most in keeping with the actual development of his thought.

2

Freud's Biography
(1856–1939)

1856: May 6, birth of Sigismund Freud (he changes his given name to Sigmund in 1878) in Freiburg in Moravia, the son of Jacob Freud (1815–1896) and his third wife, Amalia Nathansohn (1835–1930).

1873: October, enters the University of Vienna to study medicine.

1881: Becomes a Doctor of Medicine.

1882: Engagement to Martha Bernays.

1885: October 13, goes to Paris for a semester with Charcot at the Salpêtrière. Translates Charcot's *Leçons du mardi*.

1886: April, sets up medical practice in Vienna with the help of Joseph Breuer.

1887: November, meets Wilhelm Fliess, with whom he will undertake a self-analysis via correspondence beginning in April 1897.

1889: July, goes to Nancy to learn hypnotic suggestion from Hyppolite Bernheim and Ambroise Liébault. September 14, marries Martha Bernays.

1891: Publishes his first book, *Understanding the Aphasias: A Critical Study*, dedicated to Breuer. He does not retain this book among his psychological works.

1892: Treats Elisabeth von R. using the method of free association.

1895: September, *Project for a Scientific Psychology* (manuscript sent to Fliess). September 21, renounces the theory of seduction in hysteria. First theory of psychic functioning. *Studies on Hysteria*.

1896: First uses the word *psychoanalysis* in an article written in French. October 23, death of Jacob Freud. Begins work on *The Interpretation of Dreams*.

1897: Begins his self-analysis with Fliess ("This analysis is harder than any other" [1887–1902, p. 214]).

1899: November, *The Interpretation of Dreams* (dated 1900).

1900: August, breaks with Fliess.

1901: *The Psychopathology of Everyday Life*.

1902: October, beginning of the Wednesday Psychological Society, meeting at Freud's house. First psychoanalytic association (becomes the Vienna Psychoanalytic Society in April 1908).

1905: "Fragment of an Analysis of a Case of Hysteria" (the Dora case). *Jokes and Their Relation to the Unconscious. Three Essays on the Theory of Sexuality*.

1906: Begins the correspondence with Jung.

1907: Jung visits Freud. Begins the analysis of the Rat Man (1909a). Abraham visits Freud. *Delusions and Dreams in Jensen's "Gradiva."*

1908: February, Ferenczi visits Freud. April, First International Congress of Psychoanalysis held in Salzburg.

1909: August–September, Freud, Jung, and Ferenczi in the United States. Freud gives the five lectures comprising *On Psycho-Analysis* (1910a) at Clark University in Worcester, Massachusetts. "Analysis of a Phobia in a Five-Year-Old Boy."

1910: Begins the analysis of the Wolf Man (1918). March, Second International Congress of Psychoanalysis held in Zurich. Founding of the International Psychoanalytic Association (IPA). *Leonardo da Vinci and a Memory of His Childhood.* "'Wild' Psychoanalysis."

1911: "Psycho-Analytic Notes on an Autobiographical Account of a Case of Paranoia (Dementia Paranoides)" (the Schreber case). "The Handling of Dream-Interpretation in Psycho-Analysis."

1912: Creation of the Secret Committee of the six disciples closest to Freud (at the initiative of Ernest Jones). Freud gives them an ancient intaglio set in a ring and will give one to Marie Bonaparte. "The Dynamics of Transference." "Recommendations to Physicians Practicing Psycho-Analysis."

1913: *Totem and Taboo.* "On Beginning the Treatment." "The Claims of Psycho-Analysis to Scientific Interest" (paper presenting psychoanalysis to a scientific public in the journal *Scientia*). October 27, the relationship with Jung is broken off.

1914: "On Narcissism: An Introduction" (revision of drive theory and critique of Jung on the libido). "On the History of the Psycho-Analytic Movement." "Remembering, Repeating and Working-Through."

1915–1917: Begins the metapsychological writings (twelve planned, five eventually published).

1917: *Introductory Lectures on Psycho-Analysis. Mourning and Melancholia.*

1918: "From the History of an Infantile Neurosis" (the Wolf Man case).

1919: "Lines of Advance in Psycho-Analytic Therapy" (paper delivered to the IPA; owing to the widespread application of psychoanalytic therapy, Freud says, we shall be obliged to mix the pure gold of analysis with the copper of direct suggestion). "'A Child Is Being Beaten'" (analysis of a masochistic fantasy of Anna Freud's). "The 'Uncanny'" (on the repetition compulsion).

1920: January 25, death of Sophie Halberstadt, Freud's daughter. May, *Beyond the Pleasure Principle* (introduction of the death instinct).

1921: *Group Psychology and the Analysis of the Ego.*

1923: "Psycho-Analysis" and "Libido Theory," two papers for a German textbook on the sexual sciences. *The Ego and the Id.* April, Freud diagnosed with cancer of the upper jaw and the right side of the palate; the first of two operations is mishandled by Hajek. October, two new operations performed by Professor Hans Pichler, who operates thirty times and implants a prosthesis in the upper palate ("the monster").

1924: Break with Rank over the latter's theory of birth trauma. "Neurosis and Psychosis." "The Economical Problem of Masochism." "The Dissolution of the Oedipus Complex."

1925: *An Autobiographical Study.* "The Resistances to Psycho-Analysis." "Negation."

1926: *Inhibitions, Symptoms and Anxiety* (revision of the theory of anxiety and reply to Rank's theory of birth trauma). *The Question of Lay Analysis* (against the view that analysis is a medical practice).

1927: *The Future of an Illusion.* "Fetishism."

1928: "Dostoevsky and Patricide" (on guilt).

1930: Death of Freud's mother Amalia. Anna represents him at the funeral and in November at Frankfurt for the Goethe Prize, awarded to writers in the German language. *Civilisation and Its Discontents.*

1931: "Female Sexuality" (since he can now address this after the death of his mother).

1932: "The Acquisition and Control of Fire" (on sublimation and culture). September, "Why War?" (with Albert Einstein). Freud's books are burned in Germany. Beginning of the emigration of German, Austrian, and Hungarian analysts to the New World on account of Nazism. *New Introductory Lectures on Psycho-Analysis.*

1936: "A Disturbance of Memory on the Acropolis. (Letter to R. Rolland)."

1937: The first two essays of *Moses and Monotheism* (1939a). "Analysis Terminable and Interminable" (on the ending and the goals of analysis; debate with Ferenczi). "Constructions in Analysis" (how they stand with regard to interpretation).

1938: June 3, Freud is able to leave Vienna with his wife, his sister-in-law Minna, and his daughter Anna thanks to the American ambassador William Bullitt and Princess Marie Bonaparte. Goes by way of Paris and on June 6 arrives at a rented house in London. Then on September 20 moves into 20 Maresfield Garden (today the Freud Museum), a house set up for him by his son Ernest, an architect who had been living in London since 1933; he finds there his library and his collection of antiquities.

1939: March, *Moses and Monotheism* is published in London and Amsterdam. "The Splitting of the Ego in the Process of Defence." *An Outline of Psycho-Analysis* (unfinished). Freud dies in London on September 23 following doses of morphine administered at his request by his physician Max Schur.

Part II

Works

3

1893–1895.
Studies on Hysteria: Freudian Hysteria

During his medical studies in Vienna Freud took the courses in internal medicine offered by Joseph Breuer (1842–1925), who invented the cathartic method for treating hysterics in his private practice. Among these patients was the famous "Anna O." (Bertha Pappenheim), whose case is discussed in *Studies on Hysteria*, coauthored with Freud. In the second edition, however, published in 1909, Breuer was no longer willing to collaborate in a psychoanalytic endeavor and withdrew his chapter on theoretical considerations.

ELISABETH VON R.

We can find our way into Freud's conception of hysteria by looking at one of the patients presented in the *Studies*, Elisabeth von R. With this case, the birth of psychoanalysis as a methodology and a practice coincides with the revised view of hysteria in relation to the psychiatry of Freud's time. Freud treated Elisabeth von R. for several months in the fall of 1892. We can see *in statu nascendi* how Freud frees himself from the hypnotic method, what findings lead him to the invention of psychoanalysis, and in what terms he describes the new approach even before the word *psychoanalysis* was coined in 1896.

Elisabeth was 24 at the time. Before she met Freud, she lost her father, whose caretaker she had been; her mother underwent a major eye operation; and one of her married sisters died of heart complications after giving birth. "She seemed intelligent and mentally normal and bore her troubles, which interfered with her social life and pleasures, with a cheerful air—the *belle indifférence* of a hysteric" (p. 135; *belle indifférence* is an expression taken from Charcot, in French in the text). She was suffering from pains (*Schmerzen*) and paresthesias in her legs, especially in the right thigh. Freud quickly diagnoses hysteria, as opposed to an organic condition or a neurasthenia (a neurosis in which attention is focused on one's own pain).

SUFFERING FROM REPRESENTATIONS

In contrast to these, Elisabeth's attention was directed beyond her pain, toward the thoughts and feelings associated with it. Thus the first definition of Freudian hysteria is: suffering from thoughts and not from pain. As Freud writes in the preliminary communication to the *Studies* in 1893, "hysterics suffer mainly from reminiscences," that is, from representations (p. 7). His interest, therefore, lies in the content of the thoughts in the background of this pain. What leads him to give up the cathartic method is his belief that Elisabeth must know the basis of this suffering, and that she simply had "a secret and not a foreign body" in her awareness (p. 139). The secret reflects the composition of a story and not an external trauma that simply breaks into the psyche like a foreign body. Having set aside physical pain (*Schmerz*) in favor of psychic suffering, Freud is seeking to learn "the relation between the history of this suffering and the suffering itself" (p. 138). This is the first appearance in Freud of the expression "the history of a suffering," a suffering that is subjective, unique, and set in historical context. For the first time, too, Freud is starting with the most accessible layers of the patient's memories in order to reach the deeper ones, in accordance with the technique of excavating a buried city, an archeological metaphor that often recurs in his later work, especially in "Constructions in Analysis" (1937b).

HOUSE ARREST

The first element to emerge is Elisabeth's attachment to her father and the corresponding fact that he had put her in the place of the son he never had and in the place of a friend, in effect assigning her to house arrest, an impossible position for her. And this was what gave meaning to her constant complaint that she could not move (*sie komme nicht von der Stelle*), a reference to her abasia—her inability to walk—as well as her psychic impotence, the fact that she was unable to leave the place to which her father had assigned her. This place was not primarily a spatial one, although it was manifested in her difficulty in walking. It was essentially a psychic position, her inescapable imprisonment at her father's side by an utterance on his part that bound her to him. The outcome of the Oedipus complex is that we leave the place of the other in order to find our own place, a place that does not yet exist and that no one can point out to us.

THE QUESTION OF ORIGIN

Freud discovers the cause of Elisabeth's abasia by asking her, for the first time, about the origin of the representations that constrain and control her body: "I asked her various questions, such as what was the origin of her pains [*woher rühren die Schmerzen*] in walking? in standing? and in lying down?" (p. 150). The neurological localizations of paresthesias are no longer of interest. With this question, Freud invents a new body, the psychic body, marked and delimited by representations coming from the subject himself, representations of which he is the producer and the author. The hysteric suffers mainly from representations that stem from psychic conflicts and determine body language.

This question of the *woher*, the origin, in this case, of the subjective representations of fantasies, is one that Freud will raise again and again at different points in his work. We have the question of where babies come from in "On the Sexual Theories of Children" (1908a), and the *woher* appears when Freud wonders about the origin of some criminals' sense of guilt before the commission of a crime (1916). And he will return to it again to explore the origin of cultural malaise, the discontents of civilization, in 1930. Each time the search is for an endopsychic scenario that the subject revives, a scenario, in other words, that contrasts with any imputation of what I am according to some world view, to some Other whom I set up as my accuser. Chapter 7 of *Civilisation and Its Discontents* develops this logic in which the subject is implicated in the sense of guilt, challenging the notion of cultural malaise and privileging the malaise of the subject, the kind the subject inflicts on himself; malaise thus has a psychic origin, not a societal one having to do with a feeling of guilt. As Dostoyevsky so felicitously put it, what happens to us resembles us.

THE PSYCHIC BODY

Freud's question leads Elisabeth to recall that "the originally painful place on her right thigh had to do with the care she gave to her father." Specifically, this place was the one on which, each morning, her father had placed his swollen leg when she changed the bandages. It is in this way, Freud notes, that "her painful legs began to 'join the conversation'" (p. 148).

This is the first Freudian revolution: the body begins to speak and it is possible to listen to it. Here the body speaks about the incestuous tie to the father, which as it were psychically welded her father's leg to Elisabeth's right thigh, the source of her psychic hemorrhage and of her complaint that standing up alone was painful. And, since incest calls forth incest, her first amorous glances were directed toward her two brothers-in-law. In this sense, her lament that she was unable to move also reflected her inability to tear herself away from the world of incest, of the intimate, of the *heimlich* that had not yet become alien, the world of leaving home (*Heim*).

Finally, in his letter to Fliess of December 6, 1896, Freud (1887–1902) set forth his conception of hysteria as distinct from that of psychiatry: "Attacks of giddiness and fits of weeping—all these are aimed at *some other person*—but most of all the prehistoric, unforgettable other person who is never equalled by anyone later. . . . Attacks never seem to occur as an 'intensified expression of emotion'" (p. 180, emphasis in original). Here he broke with the traditional opinion of the Berlin psychiatrist Oppenheim, namely that hysteria is the intensification of an emotion, an opinion Freud had held in "The Neuro-Psychoses of Defence" (1894). Hysteria is no longer a discharge but a message, an appeal addressed to the Other.

4

1900.
*The Interpretation of
Dreams*: Between
Signification and Sense

His work on the psychic activity involved in the neuroses and the study of his own dreams in the course of his self-analysis led Freud not only to go back to the Aristotelian notion, summing up the thought of classical antiquity as a whole, that the dream is psychic life occurring during sleep, but also to take account of the importance of dream analysis. Thus his book is called, not *Dreams*, but *The Interpretation of Dreams*. Begun in 1896 after the death of his father, the work was completed in the summer of 1899 and, though it was dated 1900, appeared in November 1899.

This first book was the one that Freud considered his magnum opus introducing psychoanalysis as a new science, and he kept on adding to it and reworking it as it went through eight editions ending in 1929. (It was translated into French by the psychologist Ignace Meyerson in 1926.) Freud published a shorter version, *On Dreams*, in 1901; then, in 1922, he wrote "Remarks on the Theory and Practice of Dream-Interpretation," which was to be published as an appendix to *The Interpretation of Dreams*. Finally, the first of the *New Introductory Lectures on Psycho-Analysis* (1933) concerned a revision of dream theory.

METHOD

In this foundational act of a new conception of the psyche and of a new discipline, Freud felt obliged to devote the first chapter of *The Interpretation of Dreams* to a review of everything that had been written on this topic. He was thus able to go on to introduce a new method of dream interpretation.

Whereas scientists did not accept the dream as a psychic act but considered it a mere reaction to a somatic process, ordinary people and common sense have always accorded it a meaning (*Bedeutung*), even if that meaning is absurd and incomprehensible. Freud's originality lies in his belief not only that the dream can have a certain meaning on the manifest level, one that can be deciphered in a general symbolic way, but that it has a sense (*Sinn*) that can be found only as part of the chain of our psychic actions. Thus the dream can be considered a psychic activity of the dreamer, and its meaning is known only through the sense that the dreamer can give to it. The sense is not there from the outset; it has to be constructed and depends on the dreamer's activity. Yet Freud is careful to note that "each dream has at least one point that is impenetrable, as it were an umbilicus through which it takes part in the unconscious" (p. 184). Here Freud marks out the limits of any interpretation. No interpretation can be complete, because there is no absolute ground to the activity of thinking; the relation to the unknown is inherent in the very nature of thought. There will always be matter for further thinking and dreaming, in that no interpretation can be final.

The analysis of one of his own dreams enables Freud to claim in Chapter 3 that the dream is a wish fulfillment. But the dreamwork has to pass through censorship and must undergo distortions imposed on the dreamer's thinking. And so, in Chapter 4, Freud explains that the dream is the disguised fulfillment of a repressed wish. The distortion of the dream shows that the unconscious cannot be read like an open book, even in dreams. The initial distortion has to do with the dreamer's unique psychic activity: the dream involves work (Chapter 4) and is not merely given. Freud is the first to go beyond the manifest content of the dream and introduce new psychic material, the latent content or dream thoughts: "The [manifest] content of the dream seems to us to be a translation [*Übertragung*, a term that also means "transference"] of the dream thoughts: to put it another way, . . . the contents of the dream are given in the form of hieroglyphics, in which the signs must be translated one by one into the language of the dream thoughts" (p. 342).

DREAMWORK

The work of the dream is basically done via two mechanisms that stem from the primary processes of unconscious thought. The first is the work of condensation (*die Verdichtungsarbeit*). The poverty of the manifest content of the dream is due to the fact that each element of the dream contents is overdetermined, that is, represented several times in the dream thoughts, and each thought in the dream is represented by several elements in the dream. The second mechanism is the work of displacement (*die Verschiebungsarbeit*). Whereas condensation operates on the dreamer's representations and thoughts, displacement deploys a psychic force that establishes a connection between the manifest content of the dream and the dream thoughts. It effects a distortion of the unconscious wish in such a way that the wish can find a place in the dream contents. These elements—condensation and displacement, plus overdetermination—comprise the distortion (*Entstellung*) brought about by censorship, which nonetheless allows for representability (*Darstellbarkeit*), the staging of the unconscious wish in particular ways accessible to the dreamer.

Freud uses these same procedures in *The Psychopathology of Everyday Life* (1901a) to analyze parapraxes, slips, and lapses of memory, as well as in *Jokes and Their Relation to the Unconscious* (1905b). Chapter 7 of *The Interpretation of Dreams* is a summary of the first formulation of psychic functioning with the three agencies: unconscious, preconscious, and conscious. It ends with this definition of the wish at work in the dream: "By picturing our wishes as fulfilled, dreams are after all leading us into the future. But this future, which the dreamer pictures as the present, has been moulded by his indestructible wish into a perfect likeness of the past" (p. 621). The wish ignores time; like the unconscious, it is atemporal (*zeitlos*). It therefore tries over and over again to impose on the present the traces of the first experiences of pleasure harkening back to the past.

5

1905.

*Three Essays on
the Theory of Sexuality*

This book, *Drei Abhandlungen zur Sexualtheorie*, has been known in French and English as *Three Essays on the Theory of Sexuality*, but it would be more accurate to translate *Abhandlungen* as "treatises," since the German word does not have the subjective connotation of "essays" but refers to a systematic and scientific account of sexual theory, even if treatises discuss this topic in a phenomenological mode. Freud re-edited this book three times, with numerous additions especially in the editions of 1915 and 1920. In other words, we can see the importance he attached to this work, which completely revised the conception of sexuality shared by his contemporaries, including those who were interested in the deviations or diverse forms of sexuality, the forebears of today's sexologists, especially Havelock Ellis, Richard von Krafft-Ebbing, and Albert Moll. The work contains three treatises.

TENTATIVE SEXUAL INVESTIGATIONS

The first treatise deals with the sexual deviations (*die sexuellen Abirrungen*). The term *Abirrung* is understood figuratively and morally, and this has a major effect on Freud's thought. What is at issue are sexual wanderings, tentative explorations, between the primacy accorded the sexual drive and that accorded the sexual object. In this treatise, which is about to introduce something altogether new for its time, the taking into consideration of an infantile sexuality (Treatise 2), Freud calls into question the idea of a mature, genital sexuality by discussing deviations with regard to the sexual object (the source of attraction and sex appeal [Reiz]) and deviations with regard to the sexual aim (the act that brings the sex drive into play).

We may note that in his last preface, dated 1920 and responding to charges of "pansexualism," Freud sets his work in the context of the Platonic notion of Eros (p. 134). He thus situates his scientific investigation of human sexuality with reference not to an objectivizing and scientistic sexology but to Greek culture and mythology. For Greek culture privileges the drive over the object, while Judeo–Christian culture places more value on the sexual object than on the drive. And Freud locates sexual dimorphism, the man/woman distinction, with reference to the myth in Plato's *Symposium* of the originary dyad separated into two halves, male and female, to illustrate the desire of two beings to be united in love so as to refind the original completeness.

In the first section, discussing the sexual object, Freud takes inversion as his first example. Whereas other authors of his day distinguish among various types of inversion, placing absolute, bisexual, or occasional inverts as separate and isolated categories from a phenomenological point of view, he sees these as clearly forming a series. Beyond this classification of inverts, Freud rejects the notion that inversion represents degeneration—some of the most famous people, he observes, were inverts, perhaps even absolute inverts—or that it is inborn. It is, he says, an acquired aspect of the sexual drive. Thus, in the interpretation of inversion, pathological points of view have been replaced by an anthropological perspective. Basing his argument on Greek homosexuality, Freud notes that the most virile men are to be found among the inverts who fell in love not with the boy's manly nature but with his feminine psychic qualities, which proves that the sexual object is not of the same sex but is the reflection of the man's "own bisexual nature" (p. 144). This new interpretation of homosexuality enables Freud to draw a more general conclusion about the nature of sexuality: "The sexual drive is in the first instance independent of its object" (p. 148). This means that the sexual drive pre-exists the objects that it invests and even has the power of determining the invested object to some extent; here, for example, Freud endows boys with bisexual qualities sought by the man.

Deviations in Respect of the Sexual Aim

The second section of the first treatise sets out to discover the factors connecting the perversions to normal sexual life. Freud will explore "the anatomical borders of the body's geography," a translation more faithful to the spirit of this investigation than the title "Anatomical Extensions" (p. 150), which has too strong a connotation of the perverse structure it implies. By virtue of its precedence over the object, the drive overestimates the genitalia totally or partially, but not necessarily. This overestimation comes not from the object itself but from the allegiance accorded the object by the belief stemming from love. The belief stemming from love is the source of transference, the expectant belief that one can hope for salvation from the other. This entails a devaluation of the self as well as a deformation of the object, and it "helps to turn activities connected with other parts of the body into sexual aims" (p. 151). Fetishism, which Freud discusses in this section, is a good illustration of the fact that the substitute for the sexual object may have little sexual content of its own (foot, shoe, hair, lingerie).

Fixations of Preliminary Sexual Aims

The overestimation of the sexual object makes possible developmental arrest and fixation on preliminary stages on the way toward new sexual aims. The first of these stages is the pair touching/looking, or rather the sequence touching-looking. This is because sight arises from touching at the same time as it turns away from it. Sight is a sublimation of touching (this is the first time Freud uses the term "sublimation," here in 1905), one that permits access to the beauty of the body as a whole, and this leads the libido toward lofty artistic goals. But sight and the pleasure of seeing (*Schaulust*) occur in a twofold manner, with the active aim of seeing and the passive aim of being seen.

The pair active/passive goes all the way through Freud's oeuvre. At first it designates not a subjective or psychic position but the aim of an active or passive drive. Later on, in 1913, Freud will explain what he means by "active" and "passive": "What we speak of in ordinary life as 'masculine' or 'feminine' reduces itself from the point of view of psychology to the qualities of 'activity' and 'passivity'—that is, to qualities determined not by the instincts themselves but by their aims" (1913c, p. 182).

One of the modalities of the pair active/passive is the pair sadism/masochism. Here we see the pain inherent in the masochist's relation to the object and a component of aggression in the sadist's tendency to force matters so as to overcome the resistance of the sexual object. Freud restricts the term *perversion* to a type of relation in which gratification is possible only when the object is demeaned and mistreated. Perversion is thus a bond to the object that ensures the permanence of the relation, excluding any personal unpredictability on the object's part.

INFANTILE SEXUALITY

The second treatise flows logically from the first, which, discussing the vicissitudes of the sexual drives and the multiplicity of forms that the object's sexual attractiveness can take, reminded us that the child is father to the man, as Freud puts it, since the adult's sexual life derives from that of the child he was. It is therefore important to look at this matter of infantile sexuality, one that was not visible before Freud came on the scene. Freud notes this omission and remedies it in this second treatise.

From Nutritional Suckling to Erotic Sucking

It has been observed that, beyond the suckling of the breast by the child, there is an additional sucking after nutritional satisfaction. Freud calls this sucking that provides a more general gratification and can lead to orgasm *autoerotism*. Thus "sexual activity attaches itself to functions serving the purpose of self-preservation and does not become independent of them until later" (p. 182). The sexual drive is not autonomous with regard to the drives for self-preservation but is supported by them. The notion of leaning or dependence (*Anlehnung*), with the adjectival form *anaclitic*, indicates that the self-preservative drives (hunger, thirst, sleep) are the prototypes of the sexual drive; the model of the aim of the sexual drive is therefore not the seeking of pleasure but the cessation of the unpleasure associated with tensions internal to the organism or the psyche. The quest for pleasure, therefore, is paradoxically marked by the accumulation of unpleasure that one must then cause to stop.

At this stage, the sexual drive does not yet know any external object, since it takes as sexual object a part of the subject's own body, for example the thumb that calms the tension of the lips. At the same time, the first phenomenon of repetition makes its appearance: the need to repeat sexual gratification, which can free itself from the pleasure of self-preservation. Nevertheless, it is the trace of this first experience of pleasure that makes possible, indeed mandatory, the repetition of the search for gratification.

The Polymorphously Perverse Child

The characteristics of infantile sexuality lead Freud to generalize about its polymorphously perverse nature. He even adds that, in the adult, "the same predisposition to all the perversions is a universal and original human trait" (p. 131). In addition to the disparity between the sexual drive and its many possible objects of investment, he also points to the total independence of the sexual drives and the erogenous zones from the partial drives. The pair touching/looking has already been noted, but Freud mentions cruelty as an even greater mark of independence with regard to sexuality. This kind of cruelty takes the form of a drive to mastery in which one inflicts suffering on, or even destroys, the other or seizes objects in a clastic way, in order to destroy them, as a first mode of knowledge. This is a feature of the developmental phase in which the child is unable to empathize or identify with the other.

Infantile Sexual Investigations

Just as the sexual drives are not originally separate from self-preservation, the drive for knowledge is not independent of other drives, especially the partial drives, though these are mostly detached from the sexual drives. It is an offshoot of the drive for mastery that breaks the world in order to know it, and it works together with the pleasure of seeing, which is itself derived from touching as another mode of knowledge for the child, though at a distance and without physical contact.

Moreover, the child's investigations are bound up with egoistic and narcissistic interests in finding an answer to the enigma of origin ("Where do babies come from?"), a question formulated in the paper "On the sexual theories of children" (1908a) and taken up again in the Leonardo study (1910b). The answer to this question, which has to do with sexual difference and the place of the child in a family, assigns to the drive for knowledge the task of averting the return of events that are feared; in other words, the arrival of other children puts at risk the position of the child in his family.

The answer to the question of origin is threefold. The child formulates a sequence of three theories, these being prefantasmatic organizations aimed at providing a partial answer by elaborating the body image. The first of these theories is that of the woman with a penis, the hermaphroditic theory arising from the fact that the little boy, basing his knowledge on his own body, attributes a penis to both sexes. The second, in the ignorance of the vagina, is the cloacal theory according to which the baby is evacuated like excrement: it is a fragment of the body, not a separate body, lodged within the mother. This theory arises from the inability to conceptualize two bodies and two psyches; it remains in the register of unity with the mother. The third theory, the sadistic interpretation of coitus, indicates that the child cannot yet elaborate the difference between men and women but instead sees this in terms of a distinction between strong and weak, active and passive, sadism and masochism. These theories are developed in solitude, apart from grownups, and are a stage in a process of separation from the thought of adults, first of all the child's parents.

THE REWORKING AT PUBERTY

The third treatise broaches the topic of the later libidinal modifications of this period; they are taken up in the chapter on narcissism. Here we shall focus on the section on the discovery of the object, or, more accurately, the finding of the object.

Freud divides this process of finding into three phases. In the first, corresponding to the oral stage, the child's sexual drive finds in the maternal breast the first object external to its own body. This becomes *the lost object* when the child substitutes its thumb in the stage called autoerotic. Finally, the third phase is that of refinding an object. The loss of the object, constituting the lost object as a trace of that first experience of pleasure—indeed, as Freud puts it, "a child sucking at his mother's breast has become the prototype of every relation of love"—is, however, associated with the constitution outside the child "of a global representation of the person who possessed the organ bringing him satisfaction" (p. 222). In the mother–child (breast–mouth) relation, a double register is in play for both parties. The mother's tenderness and her care for the child's body are sources of gratification that arouse the child's sexual drive. As for the mother, her tender care for the child refers to a more sexual dimension: she "treats him as a substitute for a complete sexual object" (p. 223). This arousal places the child, at puberty, in an eminently active position for refinding, as a substitute for the lost object, an object that can bring back the lost happiness. In Freud's view, any object can substitute for another insofar as it is thought to bear traces of the lost object: "the finding of the object is in fact a refinding of it" (p. 222).

6

1910–1913.
From Transferences
to Transference
Neurosis

We can reconstruct Freud's thinking on the subject of transference by noting benchmarks that show both the chronology of his attempts at a theory and the evolution of his thought. To sum up his view, transference preexists the objects that it institutes. It is in essence a confusion between self and other according to a hysterical model, a slow, hesitant process of exchange between the identificatory register and the register of investment (the term used in the *Standard Edition* is "cathexis"). This is precisely where the hysteric is stuck: whether a man or a woman, the hysteric identifies with the person whom he or she invests.

TRANSFERENCE AND HYSTERIA

For Freud, the transference is basically a hysterical phenomenon. His originality lies in having worked out a theory not of transference but of transference neurosis. In his first formulation of the transference (1905d), Freud calls it devout expectation, in other words, a matter of faith, of belief.

This is his initial attempt at formulating the means by which certain forms of pathology can be cured at a time when he is still using hypnosis. His definition of transference is as follows: "The psychic state of expectation, which is able to set in motion an entire series of psychic forces and has the greatest effect on initiating the cure of organic conditions, is highly deserving of our interest. Anxious expectation [*ängstliche Erwartung*] is certainly not indifferent with regard to the outcome of the illness" (Breuer and Freud 1893–1895, p. 194). A little further on, he distinguishes between the physician himself and the patient's investment of him by introducing the concept of the third person. This is the missing interlocutor to whom the patient is trying to send a message but whom she assimilates to the doctor. Although he is aware of this, Freud still gropes around in his analytic practice, for example with the Rat Man (1909a), who assigns Freud the role of the cruel captain: "He repeatedly addressed me as 'Captain,' probably because at the beginning of the hour I had told him that I myself was not fond of cruelty" (p. 169). Here we can see how the Rat Man, the analysand, puts the analyst back in his place: he was not interested in speaking to Freud, but he came there to meet up again with the cruel captain with whom he had quarreled.

DISPLACEMENT OF THE OBJECT

Let us go on to "The Dynamics of Transference" (1912a) to see how, in the transference, the analysand necessarily attempts to displace the object: "How does it come about that transference is so admirably suited to be a means of resistance?" (p. 104). In this technical paper, Freud identifies transference with resistance: "It might be thought that the answer can be given without difficulty. For it is evident that it becomes particularly hard to admit to any proscribed wishful impulse if it has to be revealed in front of the very person to whom the impulse relates. Such a necessity gives rise to situations which in the real world seem scarcely possible. But it is precisely this that the patient is aiming at when he makes the object of his emotional impulses coincide [*zusammenfallen*] with the doctor" (p. 104). The patient displaces the object and tries to be as one with the analyst.

TRANSFERENCE AND REPETITION

It is clear that what the analysand wants at first is to see this relationship as a real, current one: the analysand "repeats instead of remembering, and repeats under the conditions of resistance" (1914c, p. 151). But what, exactly, is he repeating or enacting? What the patient sees as real and current in this dimension of object displacement, of object relation with the analyst, must be brought back to the past by the analyst. And here we are clearly dealing with the issue of transference neurosis. Several pages further on, Freud describes it as the patient's "replacing his ordinary neurosis by a 'transference neurosis' of which he can be cured by the therapeutic work. The transference thus creates an intermediate region between illness and real life through which the transition from the one to the other is made. The new condition has taken over all the features of the illness; but it represents an artificial illness" (p. 154). The analyst can handle transferences only to the extent that he assumes that what the patient is feeling as real and current pertains to the past and must be transformed into a transference neurosis. The transference neurosis is in some sense an interface that facilitates communication between the illness and real life.

TRANSFERENCE AND RESISTANCE

Freud identifies transference with resistance because, for him, resistance is resistance to remembering, that is, to putting an experience into its correct temporal context, assigning a date in the past to events that arise in the course of the analysis. This misrecognition of real life in the illness known as transference neurosis blurs the sense of time. In the following passages we see how Freud conceptualizes this neurosis: "It is true that in the earliest days of analytic technique we took an intellectualist view of the situation. We set a high value on the patient's knowledge of what he had forgotten, and in this we made hardly any distinction between our knowledge of it and his" (1913b, p. 141). He gives the example of a knowledge imparted from without on the basis of information gathered from parents of patients.

DISPLACEMENT OF THE REPRESENTATION

From now on, this difference between what the analyst knows and what the patient knows makes the transferential relation no longer a simple object displacement in which the analyst becomes the patient's love object as a result of transference love. We are now dealing with another relational mode, one whose essential feature is a displacement of the representation. The analyst, as third person, is the support of what gets compulsively repeated within the analytic space as representations of scenes and situations from the past. The axis of the transference now involves not the object but time.

7

1914.
On Narcissism:
An Introduction:
The Revision
of Drive Theory

HISTORICAL BACKGROUND

Before writing this 1914 paper, whose title indicates that a new conceptualization is being introduced into psychoanalytic theory, Freud paid special attention to clinical observations of the investment of one's own body, or one's own self, in narcissistic pathologies and in the origin of homosexuality. He spoke on this subject at the November 10, 1909 meeting of the Vienna Psychoanalytic Society at which Isidor Sadger presented a case of homosexuality (Nunberg and Federn 1962–1975). On this occasion Freud offered a theory of narcissism as a normal process, a necessary developmental stage in the transition from autoerotism to object love. He returned to this topic in *Totem and Taboo* (1913a), where narcissism characterizes the omnipotence of the thinking of primitive peoples and corresponds to the animist phase of cultural history. In the meantime, Otto Rank had published a paper dealing with literary examples of secondary narcissism.

As for Freud's study, besides a theoretical account of drive theory it involves a political dimension: a critique of Jung's theory of the libido. Ultimately Freud decided in favor of the term *Narzissmus* instead of *Narzississmus*; as he told Ernest Jones (1955, p. 426), he did not like the way the latter word sounded. But we can also see here the introduction of a new conception of narcissism, one that emphasizes its originality by a terminological differentiation.

AGAINST JUNG'S INTROVERSION OF THE LIBIDO

Along with the Zurich school and its leader, Ernst Bleuler, Jung had formed a theory of schizophrenia. This illness, which Freud prefers to call paraphrenia, is marked by a withdrawal of investment from reality and the external world and by hallucinations and delusions of grandeur associated with an inner feeling that the world is coming to an end. Setting out from a monistic conception of a libido that is only sexual, Jung interpreted this retreat from investment as an "introversion" of the libido. In "Transformations and Symbols of the Libido" (1912), he stated that the introversion of the Freudian sexual libido in favor of an investment of the ego could not produce the loss of reality and the sense of the end of the world that is observed in schizophrenia. On this basis he disqualifies the theory of sexual libido as providing an understanding of the neuroses.

This is the point of departure for Freud's study, a frontal attack on the work of Jung, with whom he had just broken off relations in October of 1913. For Freud, it is not possible to speak of introversion of the libido except with reference to the transference neuroses (hysteria, obsessional neurosis) but in no case for the narcissistic neuroses (Kraepelin's *dementia praecox*, Bleuler's schizophrenia, Freud's paraphrenia, and the paranoias). In paraphrenia (that is, schizophrenia in Bleuler's terminology), the libido "that is liberated by frustration does not remain attached to objects in phantasy but withdraws onto the ego" (Freud 1914a, p. 86). Delusions of grandeur correspond to the self-cure of the feeling that the world is about to end because this libidinal mass turned back on the ego is detached from any fantasy object.

We must note that the tripartite classification in use today—neurosis, psychosis, perversion—is not directly present in Freud's work, since it is too close to a psychiatric semeiology. More interested in the modalities of psychic functioning than in psychopathological structures, Freud distinguished between the transference neuroses (hysteria, obsessional neurosis, phobia) that can be treated psychoanalytically and refer back to psychic conflicts and a repressed infantile neurosis; the narcissistic neuroses (schizophrenia, paranoia) that are unlikely to lead to an analytic transference reproducing infantile conflicts in the treatment; and, finally, the actual neuroses (anxiety neurosis, neurasthenia) that are marked not by infantile or longstanding psychic conflicts but by an actual complaint with a strongly somatic component.

A NEW THEORY OF DRIVES

The ego into which the libido withdraws is a primitive one, archaic, anterior to any object relation; it is in the register of the self (*Selbst*), of the self-feeling and self-esteem that underlie the pre-objectival sense of identity. Freud calls it primary narcissism. In introducing it, he reorganizes his theoretical construction of the drives. At first he had contrasted the self-preservative drives (hunger, thirst, sleep, physical gratification), or the ego-drive, on the one hand, and on the other hand the sexual drives that stem from the self-preservative ones and are dependent on them. But the definition of the *Three Essays* (1905c), according to which breastfeeding is the model for all love relations, undermines a strict contrast between the two categories of drives, since this first relation of two functions, two part objects (mouth and breast) is what organizes the child's psychic body and its ego as a psychic envelope. Thus, alongside the ego- or self-preservative drives, we have to distinguish between an ego libido and an object libido.

The ego libido is objectless. It corresponds to primary narcissism in that it bathes the child in its mother's narcissization of it as her psyche in-forms that of her child. It is a normal stage in which there is only one psyche for two bodies. The differentiation of the child from the mother (two psyches for two bodies) comes about only with auto-erotism, constituted by the substitution of the thumb for the maternal breast, the moment at which, in this object loss, the child can form the global representation of the person whose organ brought gratification. As for object libido (secondary narcissism), it implies the constitution of this total ego (*Gesamtich*): it can invest external objects or fantasies based on them, or it can return to the ego without losing the connection to the external world. The ideal ego (*Idealich*) arises from the infantile ego that is the legacy of primary narcissism, whereas the ego ideal (*Ichideal*) stems from the demands of the ego and the superego.

8

1919–1921.
Beyond the Pleasure Principle and the Repetition Compulsion

The idea of a repetition inherent in psychic functioning, a repetition aimed at the refinding of a first experience of gratification, is found in the third of the *Three Essays*, where Freud observes that the finding of the current object is really the refinding of an original lost object. But the notion of a repetition compulsion, *Wiederholungszwang*, appears for the first time (according to a note in *SE* 12:146) in a paper on psychoanalytic technique, "Remembering, Repeating and Working-Through" (1914c). And Freud adds that the greater the resistance, the more remembering is replaced by action, emphasizing the equation he is making between action and the repetition compulsion.

THE CHOICE OF THE THIRD

But as early as 1913, a paper had prefigured the ineluctable force leading man to choose fate unbeknown to him. "The Theme of the Three Caskets" (1913d), analyzed in Shakespeare as well as in mythology, confronts man with the choice (among three caskets of gold, silver, and lead in *The Merchant of Venice* or among three daughters in *King Lear*), a choice always made in favor of the third, that is, death. Freud goes on to explain that choice replaces necessity or fatality: "In this way man overcomes death, which he has recognized intellectually. No greater triumph of wish fulfillment is conceivable. A choice is made where in reality there is obedience to a compulsion [*Zwang*]" (p. 299).

This is a situation marked by a sense of the uncanny. *Unheimlichkeit*, the German word for uncanniness, comes from the word for home, *Heim*, plus the negative prefix *un-*, referring to the censorship or repression of the first familial relationship that, later on, has become unbearable. It is an experience of something familiar that has become alien. The expression had appeared a year earlier in Chapter 3 of *Totem and Taboo* (1913a) in connection with the omnipotence of thought; Freud observes that, having turned away rationally from the animistic mode of thought, we experience it as uncanny. The situation of the familiar that has become alien ultimately leads Freud (1913d) to the three women a man meets in his life: his mother herself, his lover chosen in her image, and the earth-mother who welcomes him back to her bosom. It is as though this compulsion mysteriously at work in man prevents him from ever escaping the mother and the maternal, the original source of this "familiar turned strange."

THE "UNCANNY"

In 1919, Freud began writing two texts, "The 'Uncanny'" (1919c), which appeared in September of that year, and *Beyond the Pleasure Principle*, published in 1920. In the earlier paper, he surveys dictionaries of ancient and modern languages on the concepts *unheimlich*, the uncanny, the familiar become strange, and *heimlich*, familiar, concluding that what is *unheimlich* refers to everything that had to remain secret and emerges from the shadows, while *heimlich* evolves in the direction of an ambivalence and untimately coincides with its contrary, *unheimlich*. He goes on to review literary studies of the double, a figure who is an assurance against the disappearance of the self but becomes the disturbing herald of death, or the element of unintentional repetition encountered by Freud himself when he saw courtesans in a street in Italy and experienced a feeling of infantile distress and the familiar turned strange.

This leads him to detect the predominance of a repetition compulsion emanating from the drives beyond the pleasure principle, one that lends a "daemonic character" to life (1919c, p. 238). The word "daemonic" must be emphasized, since every repetition compulsion refers to this strangeness of the familiar. Animism, omnipotence of thought, the relation to death, unintentional repetition, and the castration complex are all factors that transform anxiety into a sense of uncanniness insofar as they all refer to the loss of ego boundaries and the anxiety of over-closeness to the maternal element, indeed to the fantasy of "intra-uterine existence" (p. 244).

In the final section of this paper, Freud draws some conclusions from what he has said, the first of these being the intellectual insecurity brought about by the infantile anxiety resulting from aloneness, silence, and darkness.

BEYOND THE PLEASURE PRINCIPLE

The third great text dealing with the repetition compulsion is *Beyond the Pleasure Principle*, begun in 1919 at the same time as "The 'Uncanny'" and published in September of 1920. Freud always denied the role of a subjective element in the final edition of this study, though a look at the manuscripts and early versions of this text reveals that the long Chapter 6, in which the concept of the death drive appears for the first time, was not written until May 1920, following the death of Freud's daughter Sophie Halberstadt on January 20 of that year and the death, at the beginning of January, of his friend and mentor Anton von Freund, publisher of psychoanalytic works (on the genetic critique and the manuscript study, see Grubrich-Simitis 1997, pp. 227–239).

"The 'Uncanny'" and *Beyond the Pleasure Principle* were written after World War I, which ravaged Europe and destroyed a form of culture, shattering nations that were fragmented or underwent a change of government. A certain Freudian pessimism was heightened: happiness is not a cultural value, he writes in *Civilisation and Its Discontents* (1930).

Beyond the Pleasure Principle has seven parts. Chapter 1 deals with pleasure (*Lust*) and unpleasure (*Unlust*) and reminds us that the pleasure principle is a mode of the psyche's primary process taken over by the self-preservative drives, the ego-drive, and the reality principle so as to obtain pleasure. But pleasure and unpleasure as conscious feelings are thus connected to the ego.

THE *FORT-DA*

Chapter 2 discusses a current issue, the war neuroses, and analyzes a child's game. The traumatic neuroses of the day were associated with the World War, on which a collaborative work by Ferenczi, Abraham, and Jones, with a preface by Freud, was published in 1919. Patients suffering from war neuroses seem to be fixated on the trauma, which does not take up time during the day but returns at night in the form of nightmares having to do with the unpleasant situation, nightmares that are broken off as the patient awakes. Here Freud proposes "to leave the dark and dismal subject of traumatic neurosis" (1920, p. 14), apparently forgetting that *The Interpretation of Dreams* (1900) had explained nightmares as not being an exception to the tendency of the dream to fulfill a wish, since one dreams of the traumatic situation in order to master it and to suppress or interrupt it by awakening. A strange lapse of memory on Freud's part!

He goes on to the game played by his little grandson Ernst Wolfgang Halberstadt, the son of the recently deceased Sophie. Freud had observed this famous game, known as the *fort-da*, a game that had two phases, each of which dealt with the passage from passivity to activity in two ways. When his mother was absent, little Ernst did not cry but threw all his toys far away while uttering the sound O-O-O, which stands for *fort* (far away, gone, absent). Ernst happened to have a spool attached to his crib by a string, and he would play at throwing it away while saying O-O-O and then gather it back with a happy *da* (there, present).

The game as a whole marked the disappearance and return of the object. In the first phase, the drive for mastery led the child to throw his toys far from him to make them absent from him as his mother absented herself from him, actively mastering her absence. In the second phase, the *fort-da* game, Ernst no longer needed to throw (and break) objects representing his mother; he could master the absence of the object in this repeated game of absence/presence. He was able to do without the object by constituting it as the lost object, passing from the absence of the object to the ability to absent himself from it.

Under the influence of the pleasure principle, it becomes possible to transform the experience of unpleasure through a psychic process that Freud calls overcoming (*Bewältigung*) set over against the drive for mastery (*Bemächtigungstrieb*) that involves mistreating the object in a clastic fashion when one is unable to separate from it or endure the absence it represents. Thus repetition here seems to be in the service of the pleasure principle.

TRANSFERENCE AND REPETITION

Chapter 3 deals with repetition in analytic treatment, first discussed in "Remembering, Repeating and Working-Through" (1914c). The patient relives a piece of his forgotten life. The therapeutic goal is reached when, as Freud had said in the earlier work, the analyst assigns to the past what the patient experiences as real and current. The patient's unconscious pushes him to reproduce scenes from the past in the present situation despite whatever repression may have been operating. The resistance to the upsurge of a past that, however pleasant back then, may be unpleasant now, comes not from the repressed unconscious but from the conscious ego in the service of the pleasure principle. What psychoanalysis reveals is that this tendency to repeat, determined by influences from early childhood, has a demonic character. Here is the term—not at all common in Freud's work—that he had used the previous year in "The 'Uncanny.'" This "compulsion to repeat" (p. 150), therefore, seems to be prior to the pleasure principle.

SPECULATION

Freud refers to Chapter 4 as speculation, explaining that "the reader will consider or dismiss this speculation according to his individual predilection" (p. 40). In reality, this chapter deals with a metapsychological construction, not a speculative one in the philosophical sense of the term. Freud discusses a theme to be developed later in *The Ego and the Id* (1923c) but already present in Chapter 7 of *The Interpretation of Dreams* (1900). Consciousness is a function of the system perception-consciousness (Pcpt-Cs), which qualifies the sensations we experience, differentiating those that come from without and those that arise from within. This system represents a boundary and filter between outside and inside that serves to mitigate external excitations and prevent them from irruption into the psychic apparatus in the form of unpleasure. But the way in which we deal with uncontrollable internal excitations is to treat them as though they did not arise from within, that is, by deploying the mechanism of projection. Finally, returning to the war neuroses, traumatic dreams, and anxiety dreams, Freud departs from the position he had taken in Chapter 4 of *The Interpretation of Dreams* and maintains that the repetition compulsion represents a "beyond" of the pleasure principle.

Chapter 5 examines drive phenomena in primitive life forms and offers very general biological and metaphysical considerations: "*The aim of all life is death*" and "*inanimate things were there before living ones*" (p. 38; emphasis in original). This recourse to the biological in introducing the concept of death is surprising; it is based, Freud says, on suppositions and deductions. He is thus led to biologize the drives: "An instinct is an urge inherent in organic life to restore an earlier state of things" (p. 36).

Finally we come to Chapter 6, dating from May 1920, in which, following the discussion in the previous chapter of the death of organisms, Freud establishes a contrast between the ego drive (of death) and the sexual drives (of life), a contrast that, he says, has no scientific basis: it is not so much a hypothesis as a belief (*Glaube*, an act of faith). Let us look at the passage as a whole:

> If we are to die ourselves, and first to lose in death those who are dearest to us [an obvious allusion to the death of his daughter, Sophie] it is easier to submit to a remorseless law of nature, to the sublime ᾿Ανάγκη [Necessity], than to a chance which might have been

escaped. It may be, however, that the belief in the internal necessity of dying is only another of those illusions [cf. Freud's ideas on the function of religion] which we have created ['to bear the burden of existence']. [p. 45 and note 1]

There is a strange trajectory in these three works, "The Theme of the Three Caskets," "The 'Uncanny,'" and *Beyond the Pleasure Principle*. The repetition compulsion loses its initial role of refinding the traces of the first experiences of pleasure and takes on a new dimension. This dimension arises from a metaphysical perspective on the field of biology and the surprising affirmation of a tendency to suppress endogenous excitation in which we find "one of our strongest reasons for *believing* in the existence of death instincts" (1920, p. 56; emphasis added). This is Freud's affirmation of a belief accompanying the return to a childhood experience with his mother, related in *The Interpretation of Dreams*:

When I was six years old and was given my first lessons by my mother, I was expected to believe that we are all made of earth and must therefore return to earth. This did not suit me and I expressed doubts of the doctrine. My mother thereupon rubbed the palms of her hands together—just as she did in making dumplings, except that there was no dough between them— and showed me the blackish scales of epidermis produced by the friction as a proof that we were made of earth. My astonishment at this ocular demonstration knew no bounds and I acquiesced in the belief which

I was later to hear expressed in the words '*Du bist der Natur einen Tod schuldig*' [Thou owest Nature a death]. So they really were Fates that I found in the kitchen when I went into it—as I had so often done in my childhood when I was hungry, while my mother, standing by the fire, had admonished me that I must wait till dinner was ready. [1900, p. 205 and note 2]

This combination of metaphysical considerations on biology and the recourse to myth leads Freud to identify woman, the mother, and death as elements of the recurrence of the demonic throughout these three texts. The only way we can bear the death of someone close to us, given the riskiness of existence, is to transform it into a strictly biological necessity inherent in the organism. At this point in his work, Freud cannot represent either death or woman directly in the notion of the deadly mother; he negates the representation of death by internalizing death. In the later analytic tradition the death drive is considered by many to be a theoretical impasse in which Freud could not separate woman from the mother who was, for him, always deadly. These writings reveal the subjective and personal factor in psychoanalytic texts.

9

1924.
Masochism and the
Meaning of Repetition

In what way is masochism a "solution" to certain problems? Freud attempts to explain this by distinguishing among primary, secondary, moral, erogenous, and feminine masochisms at the same time as he finds a common meaning to masochism in general. He explores this issue in "The Economical Problem of Masochism" (1924b), once more investigating the origin and the significance of drives after the introduction of the death drive.

THE ORGANIZATION OF THE DRIVES

We must keep in mind the organization and construction of the drive mechanism in Freud. For him, drives—beginning with eating, drinking, and sleeping—are not necessarily sexual, and the sexual is always grafted upon, linked with, supported by, and based on the drives. Hence the category of partial drives, connected with organs and in this case with specific orifices that have no sexual aim. Masochism, then, can occur in a sexual mode or a nonsexual one.

Given this fact, let us begin by considering the pair active/passive and the first two organizations of the body, the oral and the anal-sadistic, which are not orginally sexual in nature. The oral organization, in its cannibalistic aspect, seeks to make two into one, that is, to ingest and incorporate the other. The taking in of milk, the mouth–breast encounter, is the first model of the encounter with the outside world. Ingestion, incorporation, and destruction, taking from the other in order to make it into the self: this is ultimately the model for all identifications. The second organization, the anal-sadistic, does not operate in the intersubjective space, in the coming together of two organs representing parts of two different bodies, the mouth and the breast. It is a diffraction to the breast from one's own body with a double polarity, active (masculine) and passive (feminine).

The anal-sadistic organization is one of the modalities of the drive for mastery. The establishing of a muscular apparatus that precedes the conceptual apparatus (Freud 1939a) serves to gain control over an internal, erogenous mucous membrane, the intestinal mucous membrane, that at this moment, for the still inchoate body–psyche, seems to have a passive aim. The first occurrence of the drive for mastery has to do with the muscular apparatus and hence with mastery of the internal.

SADOMASOCHISM

Thus sadomasochism is initially exercised on one's own body, via the musculature, in the service of mastering an internal erogenous organ, the anal zone: the first active/passive dimension appears intrasubjectively, not intersubjectively. The drive for mastery, still not sexual, can also be transformed into a drive for destruction. In the *fort-da* game (1920), Freud's sixteen-month-old grandson, observed by his grandfather, puts two dimensions into play. On the one hand, breaking things by throwing them far away is a means of coming to know in the very act of breaking. This first mode of knowledge for the psyche consists of breaking the external world—but breaking it in order to know what? In order to know, and hence to master, connectedness or the loss of connectedness, since the game with the spool refers to the absence of the mother.

The second aspect of this drive for mastery, the destructive element, is a drive that, beyond the breaking of the other and the external world, works on the absence of connection. The only way we can put an end to our dependence on the external object is to come into our own independence. This opens out onto the phase of autoerotism, in which we recreate the active/passive relation on our own body, becoming independent of the object as the thumb and soft toys replace the breast. This independence is gained by splitting the self into two and, in an act of mastery, calming the distress stemming from passivity.

These are the initial outlines forming the basis for developing a masochistic solution as a way of escaping the other. The first theme is the active/passive pairing that Freud discusses in "The Claims of Psycho-Analysis to Scientific Interest" (1913c, referring to the interest other disciplines may have in psychoanalysis): The unconscious, he says, does not know masculine or feminine; all it knows is active and passive. This is because neither masculinity nor femininity, which have to do with anatomical differences, can be directly inscribed as representations in the psychic apparatus. In other words, the first thing the unconscious knows is the aim, active or passive, of certain drives.

INFANTILE SEXUAL THEORIES

This brings us to "On the Sexual Theories of Children" (1908a), these theories being the first elaborations of the body/psyche. I shall summarize them briefly, since they are in some sense pre-fantasies. Three in number, they are typical and are found in every psychic organization as modalities through which the growing child becomes aware of its body (the child, *das Kind*, is neuter in gender, neither boy nor girl). As we have seen, the function of these theories is to avert the risk of distress, abandonment by the object, and loss of the object.

The first cognitive activity to develop is tied to the body's component instincts and dependent on them. This initial theory, the woman with a penis, found in the mythology and sculpture of classical antiquity (hermaphroditic statues in the Louvre, Rome, and elsewhere), is that there is no sexual difference: the body knows no void, no hole—the theory being independent of the ignorance of the vagina, which is the later form of knowledge that can be held concerning the body without a hole—and this refers precisely to the musculature, the muscular body, the body-as-armor protecting us from any irruption from without.

The second sexual theory, which logically follows from the first, is the cloacal theory of birth. What is at stake in thinking of the baby as being evacuated like a stool is this: the baby is not a foreign body contained within another body but is a body fragment "shat out." The body image in this second theory once again involves the denial of separation; Freud gives the example of a mentally ill patient who showed him her excrement from the preceding day and said it was a child she had made.

In the manic state, no distinction is made between self and other, one's own thoughts and those of someone else. The third sexual theory, where we once again find the pairing active/passive but no longer as an intrapsychic feature, is the sadomasochistic theory of coitus. Here the register active/passive is first of all a contrast between strong and weak, aggressor and victim. These successive constructions of the body are worked out by the child's psyche and inscribed in the imago of the fantasized body. They are the only way in which the psyche can know the body, with no external influence but just that of the sexual drive components.

THE DRIVE TO KNOW

Hence the drive to know, with its aim of warding off feared events, is the first modality used to defend against the absence of the other, at the same time that it is dependent on these drive components and unable to anticipate the answers it will give to the successive states of the child's body. In addition, this drive to know is in the service of mastery, on condition that there is no inhibition and no external constraint. Freud essentially defines inhibition as obedience to the father, to the knowledge of the other, a subjection found later in all transferential situations. As long as we are dependent with regard to the other who is sending messages to be decoded, we cannot experience ourselves as interpreters of the other's knowledge as opposed to being subject to that knowledge. The drive to know thus provides a certain mastery, enabling us to become autonomous from the other as long as we are not hampered by inhibition in the form of infantile dependence when it comes to the other's knowledge.

Throughout this initial manifestation of the pairings active/passive, strong/weak, masculine/feminine, and sadism/masochism, it is clear that the sexual is not yet an issue, that the body is still ignorant of sexual difference and is not yet erotically sexuated.

THE EXPERIENCE OF PLEASURE

The primordial question raised by the nascent psyche of the *infans* is how to master the experience of pleasure: how to recreate pleasurable feelings that originally come from the other, especially the first, maternal other. The second organizational principle of psychic life based on the pair pleasure/unpleasure (*Lust/Unlust*) will be interfered with by the irruption of something else, enjoyment.*

For Freud, pleasure, insofar as it is not sexual but is associated with the calming of organismic tensions, is the cessation of unpleasure. His entire model of pleasure, aimed at the relief of unpleasure, that is, of internal tensions and external excitations that must be soothed, is one of organ pleasure produced by the discharge of tension. In autoerotism, masturbation, as an organ pleasure, has precisely the aim of reducing tension and anxiety, the anxiety that, unlike fear, is without object since it involves the entire body and one does not know how to get rid of it.

In this first model of pleasure, it could be said that pleasure is objectless; it is aimed at primary narcissism and autoerotism but as yet has little to do with secondary narcissism insofar as the latter is the ability to invest and disinvest the other in a circuit between oneself and the other. The basis for this first model is physiological need, and its objectless nature provides a self-calming for the body-as-armor (the musculature) that we try to protect from all excitations coming from without, and that we try to master through internal excitations in anal-sadistic erotism. Pleasure, as cessation of unpleasure, is intrinsically ambivalent, since there is a twofold phenomenon with regard to the repetition compulsion: in order to refind pleasure, we try to create situations of excitation,

---

*Translator's note: the author uses the term *jouissance*, significant in Lacanian theory.

since the only possible pleasure is the cessation of the unpleasure of excitation. Here we have the problem of masochism, since what we are doing is bringing about excitation, tension, a disagreeable situation, in order to be able to put an end to it. It is clear that this takes place in the register of mastery, that is, of a dialectic of dependence and independence aimed at making oneself as independent as possible from others.

ANXIETY AND ENJOYMENT

This organic or psychophysical suffering is called anxiety, a state in which representations are lost. Now, the only situation akin to anxiety as loss of representations is enjoyment, which, for Freud, is not *Lust*, pleasure, but *Genuss*: enjoying the other subjectively or objectively, with an aspect of possession (seizing and taking over the other) and a juridical aspect of absolute right to enjoyment: *jus utendi et abutendi*, as Roman law puts it, using and abusing, the right to consume and to destroy something by virtue of its being my property. Hence enjoyment introduces the dimension of the other, and here we leave the theater of the body and intrasubjective masochism to find the other, who is, however, still enigmatic for us (*die Rätsel im Wesen*, the essential enigma of the other), unknown, arbitrary, the other who was at the origin of the first experience of pleasure.

The pleasure/unpleasure model is now invaded by the other as external to the psyche. As an introduction to the mysteries of enjoyment and masochism, let us review some of Freud's writings. First a brief excerpt from a well known text, Letter 52 to Fliess:

> A hysterical attack is not a discharge but an *action*; and it retains the original character of every action—of being a means to reproducing pleasure. . . . That, at least, is what it is at root. . . .
>
> Attacks of giddiness and fits of weeping—all these are aimed at *some other person*—but most of all the prehistoric, unforgettable other person who is never equalled by anyone later. [1887–1902, p. 180, emphasis in original]

This view of hysteria differs from that of nineteenth-century psychiatry, which saw hysteria as primarily an orgastic discharge of tensions. Freud, especially concerned to distinguish his position from that of the Berlin psychiatrist Hermann Oppenheim, maintains that it is not a discharge but an action, a call for help directed toward the other, who is asked to come and help relieve the infantile distress. Beyond hysteria as Freud sees it, this is the fundamental scenario of asking for love from the other, and from that first, maternal other.

ENJOYMENT AND FEMININITY

In this model of appeal to the other, we find the strong and the weak; the historical, unforgettable other; and the child who can put an end to its distress only by means of the cry that will summon the mother or mother substitute. Here anxiety is directly connected to pleasure and enjoyment, which is itself feminine in nature. Pleasure is thus a kind of horror, as in the case of the Rat Man (1909a), who leaps up from the couch when confronted with a scene that he can neither bear nor speak of, asking Freud to spare him the duty to describe it (which Freud is unwilling to do) and finally admitting to "horror at pleasure of his own of which he himself was unaware" (p. 167), an enjoyment having to do with the passive, the feminine, detailed in a Chinese torture involving the insertion of an instrument into a man's anus.

The result is that we tend to repress this agonizing enjoyment. Thus Freud speaks of repression in Draft M of May 25, 1897: "It is to be suspected that the essential repressed element is always femininity. This is confirmed by the fact that women no less than men admit more easily to experiences with women than with men. What men essentially repress is their paederastic element" (1887–1902, pp. 203–204).

What does Freud have in mind here? That everything having to do with enjoyment refers to one of two types of experience: either to the invasion of the body in the form of the horror of an unknown pleasure as in the Rat Man's anal penetration, or to the loss of subjective boundaries. To put it differently, the other guarantees the repetition of the first experience of pleasure, but at the same time he is also the locus of a deadly overflowing of pleasure. This experience is deadly in that it erases bodily boundaries through the invasion of the body–psyche, in contrast to the body-as-armor that initially protects us from excitations coming from without, the muscular body to which Freud returns once again in *Moses and Monotheism* (1939a) when he uses the metaphor of the musculature in speaking of the psychic apparatus. This flooding is also a loss of psychic boundaries in terms of the loss of mastery over representations: repeated orgasm and orgastic discharge are not enjoyment insofar as enjoyment involves loss of the boundary between self and other or loss of psychic boundaries. The register of enjoyment is not the same as the register of orgasm as organ pleasure.

PAIN

What is the experience that, averting anxiety and enjoyment as two examples of the loss of representations, can refer back to the existence of the body proper, to the musculature as the defensive model of the psyche? It is pain. Physical or mental pain involves the boundaries of the body, and we might say that the experience of pain, in which "I hurt, therefore I am" contrasts with the experience of enjoyment, in which "I enjoy, therefore I lose my firm sense of myself." At this point we are on the road to the masochistic solution; in the experience of pain, I am aware of not losing my identity and even of refinding the undifferentiated mother-child relation, either in the intrasubjective form of a mental or physical pain that I can inflict on myself or in the intersubjective form of a relation in which, in the hysterical mode of appeal to the other, I will evade the encounter with the other by making this relation a return to the mother-child model. What we have here is the fusional state evoked in mania, or relations that make it possible to avoid loving or being loved by an external object, with their risk of putting an end to the fixed subject–object tie inscribed in the psyche as the first contact between breast and mouth, mother and infant.

What distinguishes perverse masochism from the ordinary variety that permits one to avoid encountering the other is that the solution provided by ordinary masochism is never entirely successful. Perverse masochism, on the other hand, succeeds because its characteristic feature is the possibility of completely mastering the enjoyment of the other by remaining external to that enjoyment, if need be, while at the same time being in charge of it; hence the sadomasochistic rituals in which, perfectly controlling the other's pain/enjoyment, the active subject remains on the outside. And this is where paranoia comes close to the perverse structure, since the paranoiac's aim is not the enjoyment of the other but mastery over the other in one's thoughts and knowledge.

In both cases, what is sought is a fixed tie to the object. Now, the overall problem of masochism does not concern the person as a whole, at least not in the sense Freud has in mind when he says that the masochist wants to be treated as a dependent child in distress. Why does it seem so simple and evident to Freud that the masochist wants to be treated as a naughty child? The masochist's wish to be a small, dependent child in distress and, at the same time, a naughty one is non-objectival. This naughty child belongs in the category of unconscious guilt to be discussed later on.

ORDINARY MASOCHISM

The manifestations of ordinary masochism are regression, depression, and self-devaluation, at least according to what Freud says in *Inhibitions, Symptoms and Anxiety* (1926a). These three characteristics involve ego-libido, never object-libido. There is something here on the order of the expectant belief that is the initial form taken by the transference: an inner psychic disposition of expectation toward the other and, correspondingly, what arises from a wish, as in a dream, a wish-fulfillment instead of an actual encounter with the other. This naturally leads to a distinction between the domain of the *Lustprinzip*, the pleasure principle and its quest for gratification; the domain of *Wünscherfüllung*, wish fulfillment that is the aim of the dream; and the domain of *Begierde*, desire, insofar as desire, for Freud, is not, as in Hegel, a desire for recognition by the other but desire for a sexual encounter with the other. In that sense, we must clearly distinguish between sexual and nonsexual (what I have called "ordinary") masochism. Masochism becomes truly sexual only to the extent that it becomes a sexual perversion, that is, when it combines at a single point in time pain as the ultimate form of excitation and something of the nature of organ pleasure, narcissistic organ pleasure whose aim is precisely to escape enjoyment.

10

1921.

Group Psychology and the Analysis of the Ego: A Generalized Theory of Identification

The idea of a work on crowd psychology first came to Freud in the spring of 1919. He began writing in February of 1920, although this text bears no relation to *Beyond the Pleasure Principle*, which appeared in the same year. It came out in book form in August 1921 under the title *Group Psychology and the Analysis of the Ego*. Its main inspiration is the 1895 book *La psychologie des foules* by the physician and sociologist Gustave Le Bon (see Moscovici 1981, which compares Le Bon, Gabriel de Tard, and Freud). Le Bon's work also directly influenced Lenin, Mussolini, and Hitler. In 1896 Le Bon published *Psychologie du socialisme*, which anticipates later critiques of totalitarianism and totalitarian systems. Freud's reservations about socialism and Bolshevism influenced his reading of Le Bon. He also has frequent citations, in the original English, from *The Group Mind* (1920) by the American sociologist William McDougall (1871–1938).

Although the English translation of Le Bon renders *foule* as *crowd*, Freud assimilates *crowd* and *group* to the German *Masse*, and, indeed, the most recent French translation of his works renders *Massenpsychologie* as *psychologie des masses*, mass psychology. I prefer to retain the reference to Le Bon by using *crowd*.

As I have noted, this book bears no theoretical relation to *Beyond the Pleasure Principle*, written at the same time. While in the latter work Freud explained subjectivation in terms of separation from the mother and maternal objects, in *Group Psychology and the Analysis of the Ego* he says at the outset that "the contrast between social and narcissistic psychic acts . . . falls wholly within the domain of individual psychology and is not well calculated to differentiate it from a social or group psychology" (p. 69). This work, then, has to do with the way the subject belongs to his surroundings. In what follows I shall be using the term *subject* as defined by Freud (1933): the ego (the I, *das Ich*), though in *The Ego and the Id* (1923c) the ego is conceptualized as one of the psychic agencies.

THE SOUL OF CROWDS

Chapter 2 presents the soul of crowds as described by Le Bon, the first sociologist to have spoken of a "psychological crowd." It discusses how psychology, which studies the drive impulses of an individual, can explain the entry of an individual into the ranks of a human multitude (*Menschenmenge*) and how such entry can affect that person. Moreover, "the psychological group is a provisional being formed of heterogeneous elements which for a moment are combined," and the problem with which this unity confronts Freud is that such a link could be what characterizes a group (p. 73). This is a problem for which

Le Bon has no answer. For him, the characteristics of the individual caught up in a crowd are the feeling of invincibility, mental contagion in the service of the general interest, and suggestibility with regard to the hypnotic leader.

Likewise, a key to the reading of this book is to view it not as a political essay but as an approach to understanding the "artificial crowds" within society, especially the army and the church. This seems to be confirmed by a letter to Romain Rolland:

> My writings cannot be what yours are: comfort and refreshment for the reader. But if I may believe that they have aroused your interest, I shall permit myself to send you a small book which is sure to be unknown to you: *Group Psychology and the Analysis of the Ego*, published in 1921. Not that I consider this work to be particularly successful, but it shows a way from the analysis of the individual to the understanding of society. [In Freud, E. L. (1960), p. 342]

In German the word for "society," *Gesellschaft*, refers to all forms of social life, to the individual's socialization outside the community (*Gemeinschaft*) of the family in any voluntary association, but it does not apply to the political form of a state imposed from without. This study, therefore, has to do with the mysterious processes that lead men to come together in a horde (as it happens, Freud also calls the society of psychoanalysts a wild army [*wildes Heer*] (letter to Georg Groddeck of June 5, 1917, in Freud, E. L. [1960], p. 316).

COLLECTIVE PSYCHIC LIFE

Chapter 3 presents Freud's perspective on the work of Le Bon, who is close to Freudian psychology in emphasizing unconscious psychic life marked by the collective inhibition of intellectual authority and the heightening of affectivity in a crowd. But the comparison with the psychic life of primitive peoples does not take into account the fact that society prescribes ethical norms. McDougall's *The Group Mind* (1920) makes the distinction between an ephemeral group that is a mere crowd and the organized group that can be a moral force. The chapter ends with a reference to the herd instinct as discussed by an English author, Trotter (1916). In a note to the second edition in 1923, Freud mentions a 1922 paper of the great Austrian jurist Hans Kelsen that takes issue with Freud's organic concept of society, according to which a stable crowd is not independent with respect to individual psychic processes.

SUGGESTION AND LIBIDO

Chapter 4 proposes Freud's views on the twofold observation made by Le Bon, McDougall, Trotter, and Freud himself about the psychic changes an individual undergoes in a crowd, including the heightening of affect. All sociologists interested in crowd psychology explained these phenomena with "the magic word 'suggestion'" (p. 88). Now, ever since his stay with Bernheim in 1889, Freud had felt hostile to "this tyranny of suggestion" (p. 89). Instead of explaining crowd psychology in terms of suggestion, then, Freud prefers the concept of libido, which covers all forms of love and attachment to others, to oneself, and even to concrete objects and abstract ideas: the sexual drives are at work in all these areas. Freud thus formulates "the supposition that love relationships . . . also constitute the essence of the group mind" (p. 91), because, on the one hand, the crowd owes its cohesion to Eros and, on the other hand, if the individual gives up his uniqueness on behalf of others, he does so out of love for them. Freud supports this general phenomenon of love in the larger sense by referring to Paul's Epistle to the Corinthians: "Though I speak with the tongues of men and of angels, and have not charity [love], I am become as a sounding brass or a tinkling cymbal" (p. 91).

TWO ARTIFICIAL CROWDS: CHURCH AND ARMY

All writers on crowds have distinguished a number of varieties: natural, artificial, transient, homogeneous, primitive, or organized crowds. Freud's intention is to differentiate between crowds with a leader (*Führer*) and those without one, and to do so with reference to two organized, lasting, and artificial crowds: the church as a community (*Gemeinschaft*) of believers, and the army, the military crowd.

The essence of these crowds lies in the libidinal bonds they manifest, whether brotherly love in the crowd of believers in relation to Christ as elder brother or, in the pyramidal structure of the army, the love officers bear toward their subordinates. As far as the army is concerned, the panic that can cause the group to break down involves the disintegration of the libidinal tie that unites the soldiers along with the subjective anxiety that takes hold of them when this bond is lost. In the case of disaggregation of the religious crowd, the risk is hostility toward others previously held in check by the love of Christ. Freud also notes that artificial crowds uphold love within the group and are intolerant of what lies outside it. In this context he refers to the socialist connection that seems to substitute for the religious connection, with the same risks of intolerance of outsiders.

IDENTIFICATION

Freud then addresses the libidinal bonds constituting the crowd with regard to their capacity to limit narcissistic self-love. Is self-love different in nature, or can it be transferred to the crowd? Examining this question, Freud returns in Chapter 7 to individual psychology and the issue of identification.

The first sentence of this chapter, "Identification is known to psycho-analysis as the earliest expression of an emotional tie with another person" (p. 105), basically defines identification as an investment, the affective relation to an other. Here Freud presents an initial formulation of the Oedipus complex that he would take up later in "The Dissolution of the Oedipus Complex" (1924c), which makes the distinction between identification and investment. Using the example of hysterical symptomatology in a girl who takes on her mother's cough, he suggests two possible interpretations of the cough: either it represents substituting for the mother in her relation to the father, or, as with Dora (1905a), taking on her father's cough, a hysterical choice in which, through this borrowed trait, Dora identifies with the love object. Freud notes here that, in both cases, identification involves only an *einziger Zug* (translated by Lacan as *trait unaire*), that is, a single trait of the other whom one wants to replace or whom one loves.

He goes on to describe three features of identification: an original form of an emotional bond, a regression in object choice, and the establishment of a new bond in an affective community via partial identification. As for the enigma of crowd formation, Freud offers the hypothesis that empathy (*Einfühlung*) makes it possible to take a position with regard to another psychic life. According to Robertson Smith, this form of identification is based on the recognition of a common substance and refers to the totem meal and the primitive history of the human family as reconstructed by Freud in *Totem and Taboo* (1913a). Freud's recourse to this mysterious transsubstantiation of the original familial bond is precisely what Kelsen objected to: conceptualizing society (*Gesellschaft*) in terms of community (*Gemeinschaft*) and the social bond in terms of the familial bond.

BEING IN LOVE AND HYPNOSIS

Chapter 8 analyzes the relations between the ego and the object. Let us recall that, for Freud, the state of being in love (*Verliebtheit*) is distinguished from love (*Liebe*) by its abnormality and passion (*Leidenschaft*): if the state of being in love "seems to be lacking normality, this is sufficiently explained by the fact that being in love in ordinary life, outside analysis, is also more similar to abnormal than to normal mental phenomena" (1915b, p. 168). Being in love is thus characterized by the sexual overvaluation of the object as a result of idealization in which, via narcissistic object choice, the object is treated like one's own ego. In this situation, the ego undermines itself and "the object has, so to speak, consumed the ego" (1921, p. 113), having taken the place of the ego ideal. Here, however, Freud notes a difference between identification and the state of being in love—investment or "cathexis"—a difference not found in his initial definition in Chapter 7. In identification, the partial traits borrowed from the object are introjected, to use Ferenczi's phrase, whereas in the state of being in love the opposite occurs: the ego has introjected the object in its totality.

Identification thus seems to presuppose the giving up of object investment. The question arises as to what it is in the object that is given up. In other words, we need to know *"whether the object is put in place of the ego or of the ego ideal"* (p. 114; emphasis in original). Insofar as there is the same unquestioning acceptance toward the hypnotist and toward the love object, we may conclude that the object is put in the place of the ego ideal. Aim-inhibited sexual tendencies, present in both situations, help to maintain a bond that is all the more durable for there being no sexual gratification involved. Here Freud could have referred to the phenomenon of courtly love, in which the man is bound in subjection to the lady without a sexual relationship.

Freud ends the chapter with the observation that a crowd that has a leader "is a number of individuals who have put one and the same object in the place of their ego ideal and have consequently identified themselves with one another in their ego" (p. 116). Hypnosis involves the gaze of the hypnotist (a gaze that Lacan calls *objet a*) and a radical desubjectivation. Commenting on this passage to shed light on the Holocaust and Nazism, Lacan (1964) writes as follows: "I maintain that no sense of history based on Hegelian–Marxist premises is able to account for this resurgence in which it turns out that the offering of an object of sacrifice to obscure gods is something to which few subjects can resist succumbing in a monstrous capture" (pp. 246–247, trans. S. F.). The sacrifice of subjectivity, the subjective deprivation, are in the service of crowd organization.

THE HERD INSTINCT

One of the authors studied by Freud, Wilfred Trotter, wrote *Instincts of the Herd in Peace and War* in 1916. These instincts, Trotter says, can account for the regression of psychic activity observed in a crowd, along with intellectual weakening and disinhibition of affect. Trotter derives these phenomena from a specific herd instinct because man feels incomplete, isolated, and anxious when alone. In artificial crowds organized by a leader, the human wish for equality is accompanied by the wish to be dominated by a single individual. Hence Freud emends Trotter's claim that man is a herd animal (*Herdentier*) with the following definition: "man is a horde animal [*Hordentier*], an individual creature in a horde led by a chief" (p. 121).

DESUBJECTIVATION

This horror of individuation, the wish for radical desubjectivation and melting into the anonymity of a whole so as to find strength and power there, have seldom been evoked with the clarity of T. E. Lawrence in *The Mint* (1922), a book describing his experience in the Royal Air Force in 1922 under the anonymous identity of the simple soldier Ross. Lawrence describes how the men wanted to be not individuals but a unit, so docile to their leader, so in need of a master, that they lost the power of decision. This text prefigures Freud's final reflections on the need for the crowd: "We know that in the mass of mankind there is a powerful need for an authority who can be admired, before whom one bows down, by whom one is ruled and perhaps even ill-treated. We have learnt from the psychology of individual men what the origin is of this need of the masses. It is a longing for the father" (1939a, p. 109). But here, too, it is with the categories of individual psychology that Freud analyzes the social.

11

1923.
The Ego and the Id:
Revision of the
Psychic Apparatus

HISTORICAL BACKGROUND

This small book, published in 1923, was written in the second half of 1922. Freud begins by envisioning it as a continuation of *Beyond the Pleasure Principle*, but he is careful to emphasize that he is not making any new borrowings from biology and is staying closer to psychoanalysis than in the earlier work. He also mentions that this text does not involve speculation, which suggests that *Beyond the Pleasure Principle* did just that. In contrast to *Beyond the Pleasure Principle*, which was greeted with reservations from the time of its publication, *The Ego and the Id* was well received by analysts, since it clarifies the notion of the unconscious and reorganizes the theory of the psyche.

It is also in this text that Freud moves on from the topological theory to the structural theory of the psychic apparatus. In Chapter 7 of *The Interpretation of Dreams* he had introduced a topology with three modalities of psychic functioning: unconscious, preconscious, and conscious. He returned to this spatial representation in a brief but important paper, "Formulations on the Two Principles of Mental Functioning" (1911c), in which he introduced the contrast between the pleasure principle and the reality principle and hence the contrast between the pleasure ego and the reality ego.

The pleasure principle functions according to unconscious primary processes and creates fantasies in the form of daydreams without relation to external reality. The reality principle represents the external world as it really is and aims at change in the context of that reality. The reality principle represents "the real state of the external world" and aims at a real modification. With the reality principle, "what was represented was no longer what was agreeable but what was real, even if it would have to be disagreeable." And Freud adds in a note on the same page: "The state of sleep is able to re-establish the likeness of mental life as it was before the recognition of reality, because a prerequisite of sleep is a deliberate rejection [*Verleugnung* 'disavowal'] of reality (the wish to sleep)" (1911c, p. 219, note 3). In the metapsychological papers of 1915 (1915a,c), Freud goes deeper into certain aspects of psychic functioning with discussions of repression and the unconscious. After 1923, papers that supplement *The Ego and the Id* include "Negation" (1925c), "Fetishism" (1927b), the discussion of the decomposition of the personality in the *New Introductory Lectures on Psycho-Analysis* of 1933, and "Splitting of the Ego in the Process of Defence" (1939b).

CONSCIOUSNESS AND UNCONSCIOUSNESS

In this introductory section, Freud reminds us of the foremost shibboleth of psychoanalysis: consciousness is a quality of the psyche, but it is not the whole of the psyche, which is to a large extent unconscious. Such a proposition, unacceptable to logical thought and philosophy, is the basis of psychoanalysis and is alone able to account for psychopathological processes.

Let us pause for a moment at this term *shibboleth*, which recurs several times in Freud. This word, which comes from the Old Testament, was a sign of tribal recognition when pronounced correctly. In the *Three Essays* (1905c), Freud makes the Oedipus complex the shibboleth. Shibboleths are fundamental concepts of psychoanalysis that are not exhaustive: the unconscious, repression, resistance, dream interpretation, infantile sexuality, and the Oedipus complex. They refer not to a body of doctrine but to psychic mechanisms, and it is for this reason that there is no unified theory of the psyche in Freud but only particular approaches.

Consciousness is an activity that concerns the pure present, a perception that the psyche can transform into a representation of a parcel of external reality. As soon as we pass on to another perception, that representation becomes unconscious in the descriptive sense, that is, it can be summoned up and once again made conscious. This form of unconsciousness should therefore be called preconscious. The unconscious proper is connected with repression. What is repressed is unable to become conscious again; it is by nature unconscious. Thus we have three terms: the conscious (cs), the preconscious (pcs), and the unconscious (ucs).

There is also a third form of unconsciousness (besides the preconscious and the repressed unconscious proper), one that occurs in the resistances appearing in the course of analytic treatment to ward off the memory of past experiences: this nonrepressed unconscious, associated with the resistances of the ego, is a part of the unconscious ego that is constituted by splitting: "It is to this ego that consciousness is attached; the ego controls the approach to motility—that is, to the discharge of excitations into the external world; it is the mental agency which supervises all its own constituent processes, and which goes to sleep at night, though even then it exercises the censorship on dreams" (p. 17). This clinical observation calls for a reevaluation of the relations between the ego and the id, as in the previous section.

THE EGO AND THE ID

Whereas unconscious representation is accomplished on material that remains unrecognized and therefore unknowable, preconscious representation, which is based on thinking, is associated with word representations. Hence, when a represention becomes conscious, it must pass through a relation to a word representation that is the mnemic trace of an external perception, and this in turn must pass through the filter of the ego and the system Pcpt-cs (perception-consciousness) that organizes the relation of the ego to external reality.

Internal perceptions are sensations arising from the deepest psychic layers, the ones most remote from word representations. Unlike external perceptions, these may be either conscious or unconscious, and they become conscious directly, without passing through word representations. On the basis of these definitions, Freud theorizes a new psychic apparatus: an individual is "a psychical id, unknown and unconscious, upon whose surface rests the ego, developed from its nucleus the Pcpt. system" (p. 24). The perception system is the agency of the present that filters external perceptions and transforms them into representations so that the psyche can recognize and identify them.

As for the ego, it "does not completely envelop the id," but does so only on the borders of the Pcpt. system constituting its surface (p. 24). The ego is thus not really separate from the id but is its surface, even "that part of the id which has been modified by the direct influence of the external world," that is, by culture (p. 25). The ego therefore tries to master the id on the basis of the external world through culture, morality, and the reality principle. Hence the ego can be defined as a surface phenomenon, a "body-ego" (p. 27) on the boundary between inside and outside, differentiating between internal and external perceptions. This is what projection cannot do, since it projects onto the outside feelings that the ego or the subject refuses to recognize or identify.

Freud ends this chapter with two observations: one's conscience (*Gewissen*) is unconscious, and it is possible to have an unconscious sense of guilt, which shows that both the deepest and the loftiest elements can be unconscious. Let us recall how Freud explains the difference between affect and representation: representations are cathexes, based on mnemic traces, whereas affects and feelings correspond to discharge processes whose final manifestations are perceived as sensations.

EGO AND SUPEREGO (EGO IDEAL)

But the ego is just the id's surface, not the sole representative of the external world. Freud's theory of narcissism distinguished a part of the ego that is the ego ideal or superego, the representative of culture for the ego. Moreover, in Chapter 7 of *Group Psychology and Analysis of the Ego* (1921), dealing with identification, Freud demonstrated that the first, archaic oral relations do not allow a distinction between what belongs to the register of investment and what belongs to the register of identification. It could even be said that the first forms of identification involve the fantasmatic incorporation of the other or the introjection, as permanent psychic processes, of a trait of the other (*einziger Zug*). It is in the course of these operations that sexual libido changes into object libido, narcissistic libido of the secondary narcissistic kind that flows back toward the ego when the first objects are abandoned and disinvested in favor of identifications.

The first identification occurs not so much chronologically as somehow ontologically, essentially, since it is the "identification with the father of . . . personal prehistory" (1923c, p. 31). It arises not from investment of an object but is direct, originary, the condition of possibility for subjective identity and all subsequent identifications.

The ego ideal is the cultural result of this originary identification that brought about the decline of the Oedipus complex so as to locate investments elsewhere (as will be discussed in Chapter 12).

The superego is also the result of two factors, "one of a biological and the other of a historical nature": the long state of helplessness of the child and the Oedipus complex (p. 35). Thus the ego ideal is presented as "a substitute for a longing for the father" (p. 37). We can see that, if a personal ego ideal is lacking, one can be negotiated in a group context for a common ideal. The ego ideal, finally, is the subjective, personal substitute for religion, morality, and social feeling.

THE TWO CLASSES OF INSTINCTS

In this chapter, Freud tries to connect his new theory of the psychic apparatus—ego, id, superego—with the concepts developed in Chapter 6 of *Beyond the Pleasure Principle* (1920) on the death drive alongside Eros or the sexual drives. The death drive no longer works silently but becomes "an instinct of destruction" (1923c, p. 41), even in the service of Eros for the purposes of discharge. Further on, Freud adds that "the distinction between the two classes of instincts does not seem sufficiently assured and it is possible that facts of clinical analysis may be found which will do away with its pretension" (p. 42).

And indeed, clinical experience reveals purely internal changes from love to hate with regard to an object: "The ground is cut away from under a distinction so fundamental as that between erotic instincts and death instincts, one which presupposes physiological processes running in opposite directions" (p. 43). Although clinical data cannot give an account of the two types of drive, even if instinctual impulses turn out to be "derivatives of Eros," Freud feels obliged to maintain this conception (drive duality) because "the death instincts are by their nature mute" (p. 46). In short, what we have here is the final reiteration of the act of faith posited at the end of *Beyond the Pleasure Principle*.

THE EGO'S DEPENDENCY RELATIONS

This last chapter discusses the relations of the ego to the other agencies, and their interdependence, on the basis of clinical experience. Even if the superego is the representative of culture, the outer world, and the reality principle, it is closer to the id than to the ego and is thus for the most part unconscious and contrary to the interests of the ego.

The first example Freud gives is that of the temporary deterioration of the treatment, and here he introduces the notion of the negative therapeutic reaction marked by "narcissistic inaccessibility, a negative attitude" with regard to the treatment (p. 49); he will return to the negative therapeutic reaction in "Constructions in Analysis" (1937b).

Freud explains this clinical phenomenon in terms of the sense of guilt, a concept to be developed later in Chapter 7 of *Civilisation and Its Discontents* (1930). This uncon-

scious sense of guilt is merely a borrowed feeling, the resi-
due of a bond, impossible to undo, with an abandoned love
relation. In the face of this resistance to giving up a residual
bond, Freud defines it as being inseparable from the other.
Here, in *The Ego and the Id*, he sets down a rule of technique
that may be found surprising on account of the freedom of
will and decision conferred on the patient: "Analysis does
not set out to make pathological reactions impossible but to
give the patient's ego *freedom* to decide one way or the other"
(p. 30, note 1; emphasis in original). The ego is this regula-
tory agency, evolving "from perceiving instincts to controlling them" (p. 55). Thus, according to a definition that has
been forgotten, "psycho-analysis is an instrument to enable
the ego to achieve a progressive conquest of the id," insofar
as, from Freud's point of view, the id is totally amoral (p. 56).

This formulation provides us with a better understanding of the ending of the thirty-first of the *New Introductory
Lectures on Psycho-Analysis* (1933), where Freud returns
to the schema of the psychic apparatus presented in Chapter 2 of *The Ego and the Id* in a passage that has given rise
to a number of translations and interpretations in France:
"[The intention of therapeutic effects of psychoanalysis]
is to strengthen the ego, to make it more independent of
the super-ego, to widen its field of perception and enlarge
its organization, so that it can appropriate fresh portions
of the id. Where id was, there ego shall be [*Wo Es war, soll
Ich werden*]. It is a work of culture—not unlike the drain-
ing of the Zuider Zee" (p. 80).

In a Heideggerian tonality of return to the origin,
Lacan (1977) translates: "Where it used to be, it is my duty

to come to be" (cf. p. 128), and he has also offered as a translation: "Where it was, I must come into being." These two versions run counter to Freud's intention, which is not to immerse the ego in the id once again so as to recharge it with energy but rather to dominate the id.

12

1924.
"The Dissolution of the
Oedipus Complex":
Finding One's Place

This 1924 paper brings together Freud's ideas on the Oedipus, the primary stakes of which are organizing investment and identification so as to construct a sexual identity at the time of puberty. It is the culmination of his thinking in *Group Psychology and Analysis of the Ego* (1921) and in *The Ego and the Id* (1923), which presents a new topology of psychic processes. The current French translation speaks of "the disappearance" of the Oedipus complex, but this ignores the sense of the German term, *der Untergang*. *Untergang** is used of the setting sun and of a boat sinking into the sea. The image is thus less that of a disappearance as of a passage to another position. The Oedipus complex is neither suppressed nor dissolved; it declines like the setting sun (*Sonnenuntergang*) via the repression that sends it into unconsciousness.

HISTORICAL OEDIPUS

The Oedipus complex was originally discovered in Freud himself in the context of his self-analysis, and his experi-

---

*Translator's note: *Untergang* literally means "going under."

ence enabled him to generalize it. He mentions it for the first time in a letter to Wilhelm Fliess dated October 15, 1897:

> Only one idea of general value has occurred to me. I have found love of the mother and jealousy of the father in my own case too, and now believe it to be a general phenomenon of early childhood, even if it does not always occur so early as in children who have been made hysterics. (Similarly with the "romanticization of origins" in the case of paranoiacs—heroes, founders of religion.) If that is the case, the gripping power of *Oedipus Rex*, in spite of all the rational objections to the inexorable fate that the story presupposes, becomes intelligible, and one can understand why later fate dramas were such failures. Our feelings rise against any arbitrary, individual fate such as shown in the *Ahnfrau*, etc., but the Greek myth seizes on a compulsion which everyone recognizes because he has felt traces of it in himself. Every member of the audience was once a budding Oedipus in phantasy, and this dream-fulfillment played out in reality causes everyone to recoil in horror, with the full measure of repression which separates his infantile from his present state. [1887–1902, pp. 223–224]

In this same letter, Freud analyzes Shakespeare's *Hamlet* in oedipal terms. Then, in *The Interpretation of Dreams* (1900), he returns to the Oedipus and the Sophoclean tragedy that confirms our childhood dreams and reminds us of a repressed, buried past:

It is the fate of all of us, perhaps to direct our first sexual impulse toward our mother and our first hatred and our first murderous wish toward our father. Our dreams convince us that this is so. King Oedipus, who slew his father Laius and married his mother Jocasta, merely shows us the fulfillment of our childhood wishes. But, more fortunate than he, we have meanwhile succeeded, in so far as we have not become psychoneurotics, in detaching our sexual impulses from our mothers and forgetting our jealousy of our fathers. Here is one in whom these primaeval wishes of our childhood have been fulfilled, and we shrink back from him with the whole force of the repression by which those wishes have since that time been held down within us. While the poet, as he unravels the past, brings to light the guilt of Oedipus, he is at the same time compelling us to recognize our own inner minds, in which those same impulses, though suppressed, are still to be found. [pp. 262–263]

STRUCTURAL OEDIPUS

Here Freud approaches the problem from a perspective that is no longer historical but structural, speaking from the boy's point of view and only secondarily from the girl's. He offers several hypotheses on the decline of the Oedipus, which is actually the decline of infantile sexuality and the child's exclusive love for the opposite-sex parent, after having had the mother as sole sexual object. As early as "The Dynamics of Transference" (1912a), Freud had recalled that originally "we knew only sexual objects; and psychoanalysis shows us that people who in our real life are merely admired or respected may still be sexual objects for our unconscious" (p. 105). Our unconscious preserves, in a repressed form, the traces of our first sexual investments. The decline may be due to the intrinsic impossibility of an experience of gratification from parents who turn away from their children and thereby create frustration, or the complex may be predetermined to follow an innate, phylogenetic program in all children. To these ontogenetic and phylogenetic explanations Freud adds a more recent hypothesis. Following the oral phase associated with the loss of the breast, and the anal phase associated with the loss of feces (experienced as part of one's own body), there comes a new phase, the phallic phase, that, beyond the male genital, the penis, serves as an identificatory pivot for the construction of the body after the oral and anal losses (and castrations).

THE PHALLIC PHASE

The phallic genital organization founders under the threat of castration, a threat for which the child was already prepared by the "withdrawal of the mother's breast" and the "daily demand . . . to give up the contents of the bowel" as a fantasized part of its own body (p. 175). The castration anxiety of the phallic genital organization is in some way the denial of the flesh as a possible locus of identity and a possible means of acceding to another psychic identity. The Oedipus complex for the boy thus plays out on the level of psychic locations to occupy or abandon, and this sums up Freud's theory of identification: "The Oedipus complex offered the child [*das Kind*; the word is neuter in German] two possibilities of satisfaction, an active and a passive one. He could put himself in his father's place [*Stelle*] in a masculine fashion and have intercourse with his mother as his father did, in which case he would soon have felt the latter as a hindrance; or he might want to take the place of his mother and be loved by his father, in which case his mother would become superfluous" (p. 176).

In the first scenario, the father's place with regard to the mother is taken in an active, masculine way; in the second, the mother's place with regard to the father is assumed. In both cases, the position is a hysterical or imaginary one involving both investment and identification.

THE DECLINE

The decline of the Oedipus complex, or its exit, is the time at which object investments are abandoned in favor of identification, the time, in other words, when the permutative equivalence between investment and identification, which is highly confusing for the child (I identify with the person I invest), ceases and is replaced by an identificatory process in which the child disinvests the parental imagos and identifies with an X that is his own future: when he is grown up, he will be X and do X.

The identificatory process can occur only in the psychic subjective place (*Stelle*) of the child and not elsewhere.

Freud had already broached the topic of the oedipal stakes as a cultural task for each person as well as the kernel of every neurosis in the twenty-first of the *Introductory Lectures on Psycho-Analysis* (1917a). At this time, however, the connection and the contrast between investment and identification, developed in the structural theory and in *The Ego and the Id*, was not yet a factor in the Oedipus.

13

Negation, Disavowal,
and the Activity
of Thought

Denial and disavowal are two modes of psychic activity, belatedly highlighted by Freud, that deserve attention.

NEGATION (1925C)

Few Freudian texts have been commented on by philosophers and psychoanalysts as much as the short paper "Negation," which deals with the activity of judgment—judgment of attribution and judgment of existence—and with the ability or inability to acknowledge a representation of thought as one's own. The term *Verneinung* is translated as both "denial" and "negation" (cf. Laplanche and Pontalis 1973, pp. 261–262).

In just a few pages, this paper discusses the origin of intellectual judgment, the origin of the representation, the constitution of the ego and the external object, and the recognition of the unconscious by a denial carried out by the ego (there is no "no" in the unconscious, since the unconscious knows neither time nor negation). Freud sets out from the clinical observation of an idea coming to mind (the *Einfall* or "incursion" is a thought that occurs spontaneously, without prior reflection): "You ask who this person in the dream can be. It's *not* my mother" (p. 235; emphasis in original). The analyst can conclude that it is indeed about the mother. Thus the denial refers not to the representation itself—a mother—but to the connection that the dreamer may have with it. Denial thus points the way to a repressed representation.

Freud succinctly describes another mechanism in connection with obsessive representations: a particular idea occurs to me, but "it can't be true, or the idea wouldn't have occurred to me," and Freud explains: "What he is repudiating [*verwirft*, from the same verb stem as *Verwerfung*: throws outside oneself or forecloses] ... is the correct meaning of the obsessive idea" (p. 235). Returning to denial, Freud observes that the content of a repressed representation or thought cannot reach consciousness unless it is denied. Insofar as the unconscious knows no negation, this denial allows for the becoming conscious of repressed material without the concomitant acceptance of its subjective factor. Denial clearly reveals the disjunction that can exist between the intellectual faculty of judgment and the affective process. Through denial, the repressed representation can reach awareness, but not the aspect of it that led to the repression. Here we can see the psychological origin of the intellectual function. Denial is the equivalent of a wish for repression. Thus Freud defines the twofold function of judgment: judgment of attribution and judgment of existence.

Judgment of Attribution

Judgment of attribution, affirming or disaffirming "the possession by a thing of a particular attribute" (p. 236), stems from the original oral drives: taking the good into the self and expelling the bad (1911c). And here there occurs a phrase that has led to a great deal of misinterpretation: *Das Schlechte, das dem Ich Fremde, das Aussenbefindliche, ist ihm zunächst identisch*: "What is bad, foreign to the ego, located outside, is first of all identical for it." This means that, for the pleasure-ego, what is bad, what is alien, and what is outside are the same thing for it. Unfortunately, this sentence has been translated to mean "What is bad, what is alien to the ego, and what is external are, to begin with, identical" (p. 237). If the outside, the bad, is identical to the ego, there could be no difference between the ego and an external reality so constituted. Hence the ego identified with the outside in this expulsion (*Ausstossung*) could constitute a real (in the Lacanian sense) that is forever unknowable and inaccessible. This is Lacan's interpretation in his commentary on *Verneinung*: "The expulsion outside the subject. It is this that constitutes the real insofar as the real is the domain of that which subsists outside symbolization" (1977, p. 338). But this amounts to the impossibility of differentiating between inside and outside and merely posits a subject vis-à-vis a real (which is not external reality) that cannot be symbolized. This obviously entails an entire theory of the body image.

Judgment of Existence

The second function of judgment is judgment of existence. It is based on "the definitive reality-ego which develops out of the initial pleasure-ego" (p. 237) when put to the test of reality. Here the question is no longer knowing whether a perception should be present in the ego but knowing whether it is also present in external reality. This once again raises the issue of distinguishing inside from outside. Does or doesn't a representation refer to an outside reality? "What is unreal, merely a representation and subjective, is only internal; what is real is also there outside" (p. 237). A hallucination, for example, is just a representation without an object.

Here Freud explains that, at the outset, representations arise from perceptions and are in some sense the transformations of perceptions in such a way that the representation can subsequently recognize new perceptions or external realities. Thus he notes that "The first and immediate aim . . . of reality-testing is, not to *find* an object in real perception which corresponds to the one presented, but to *refind* the object" (p. 237; emphasis in original; this is another way of recalling what he had proposed in the *Three Essays*). We can see how the activity of judgment develops from the primary drive activities of swallowing and spitting out. As for the negativism of schizophrenics, it indicates a loosening of connection among the drives. Nevertheless, the symbol of denial is the first sign of the freeing of the ego with regard to repression.

FETISHISM (1927)

The concept of fetishism was introduced into psychopathology by the French psychologist Alfred Binet in an 1887 paper on erotic fetishism, and other sexological studies at the end of the nineteenth century analyzed various aspects of this topic. Freud discusses it for the first time in the first of the *Three Essays* (1905c), defining it first as follows: the normal object "is replaced by another which bears some relation to it but is entirely unsuited to serve the normal sexual aim." He continues with the observation that the substitute for the sexual object "is some part of the body (such as the foot or hair) which is in general very inappropriate for sexual purposes. . . . Such substitutes are with some justice likened to the fetishes in which savages believe their gods are embodied" (p. 153). Whereas Binet had emphasized that fetishism might involve the urgent persistence of an infantile sexual impression, Freud, in a note added in 1920, doubts that pathological fixations can set in so late. He proposes another scenario, namely that "behind the first recollection of the fetish's appearance there lies a submerged and forgotten phase of sexual development. The fetish, like a 'screen memory,' represents this phase and is thus a remnant and precipitate of it" (p. 154, note 2).

Freud's interest in fetishism is such that he returned to it in a lecture on the origin of fetishism given before the Wednesday Society on February 24, 1909 (Freud 1909d). He describes the very odd case of a young man who spent a long time close to his mother, to the point where they undressed in each other's presence. There followed the repression of this sexual drive, though the patient adored clothing; that is, having repressed the pleasure in seeing, he worshiped what had prevented him from seeing. Freud explains that this fetishization is just an idealization, and he gives the example of the Middle Ages, in which the repression of sensuality and the degradation of women coexisted with the idealization of the Virgin Mother. Finally, in 1927, he returns to the topic of fetishism and introduces another mechanism besides idealization as overvaluation of the object: the fetish "is the substitute [*Ersatz*] for the woman's (the mother's) penis that the little boy believed in and—for reasons familiar to us—does not want to give up" (1927b, pp. 152–153).

DISAVOWAL

The child refused to become aware of the reality of his perception, and as a result he establishes a fetish so as to deny the perception of the lack of a penis in women. The French psychoanalyst René Laforgue has suggested the term *scotomization* for this denial of perception, but this is not what Freud has in mind, since what is involved is not the disappearance of a perception as in ocular scotomization. Instead, what occurs is a specific activity of the psyche, which is to interpose a monument to replace the lack of the woman's penis. The mechanism of repression, which has to do with affect, seems inadequate to Freud as a designation for this active psychic work of denying an unbearable perception.

He therefore proposes the term *Verleugnung*, "disavowal." One disavows an intolerable perception. Octave Mannoni (1969) has expressed this as "I'm well aware, but nevertheless . . ." (pp. 9–33), indicating that this is a belief that replaces a perception.

Part III

The Meaning
of Freudianism

14

The Question
of Lay Analysis:
The Status of
Psychoanalysis
in Society

HISTORICAL BACKGROUND

In "The Moses of Michelangelo" (1914d), first published anonymously in the journal *Imago*, Freud had said of himself that "I am no connoisseur in art but simply a layman" (*Ich bin kein Kunstkenner, sondern Laie*"; p. 211). The word *Laie* could also be translated as "amateur." In raising the question of lay analysis, Freud now investigates the situation of psychoanalysis among the disciplines as well as its status in society. In discussing this twofold problem, his paper takes the form of an imaginary dialogue with an impartial interlocutor. This interlocutor may be the professor of medicine Durig, a member of the medical establishment, but we may also hypothesize that he could be Professor Julius Tandler, of the Viennese Health Department, to whom Freud had written a letter on the Reik affair on March 8, 1925. Recalling their conversation, Freud wrote: "You seemed to approve of my statement that 'in psychoanalysis everyone has to be considered a layman who cannot prove a satisfactory training in the theory and technique of it,' no matter whether he has a medical degree or not" (quoted in E. L. Freud 1960, p. 359).

This letter deserves to be cited because here Freud uses the term "layman" (*Laie*) in the sense of "amateur" and juxtaposes physicians and nonphysicians in regard to analytic incompetence. In the phrase *Ich bin kein Kunstkenner, sondern Laie*, we may surely keep the term "layman," which in French is *profane*, literally "in front of the temple," in contrast to the sacred: the *Laie* as opposed to any medical or religious clergy but also in relation to the educated amateur. The occasion for the paper on lay analysis (1926b) was the action brought against Theodor Reik on the grounds of practicing medicine illegitimately. Freud wrote this work in June of 1926 and it was published in July in support of Reik.

For Freud, according to Jean-Baptiste Pontalis (1985), the question of lay analysis is the question of analysis itself. Freud is waging a twofold battle. First, he inveighs against physicians, observing that psychoanalysis is not the maid-of-all work of psychiatry. Let us recall that Freud was not a psychiatrist but a neurologist who had trained in internal medicine under Breuer. Second, he criticizes wild analysis, in which everything is interpreted right away: "I have heard that there are analysts who plume themselves upon these kinds of lightning diagnoses and 'express' treatments, but I must warn everyone against following such examples" (1913b, p. 140).

THE QUESTION OF LAY ANALYSIS

Over the course of seven chapters Freud responds to an impartial interlocutor on the issue of analysis conducted by nonphysicians. To the interlocutor's first question about what the analyst undertakes with the patient whom the physician could not help, Freud replies: "Nothing takes place between them except that they talk to each other. . . . The analyst agrees upon a fixed regular hour with the patient, gets him to talk, listens to him, talks to him in his turn and gets him to listen" (p. 187). Thus psychoanalysis is essentially a matter of speaking and being spoken to. The second chapter is a simplified account of the psychic apparatus as theorized in *The Ego and the Id* (1923c). However, this chapter ends by affirming the need for a personal analysis, so that analysts will "experience as affecting their own person—or rather, their own mind—the processes asserted by analysis" (p. 199). This appeal to personal experience is necessary in order to put to the test the theory of psychic processes.

Chapter 3, on the topic of neurosis, defines the aim of treatment: We try to restore the ego, to free it from its restrictions, and to give it back the command over the id which it lost owing to its early repressions" (p. 205), a formulation that anticipates the famous saying, *Wo Es war, soll Ich werden*, "Where It [the id] was, I [the ego] should come into being." Chapter 4, the longest, has to do with the sexual factor in the neuroses, infantile sexuality, and the role of sexuality in analytic treatment. Chapter 5 points out that medical training is of little importance in clinical psychoanalysis. Psychoanalysis is a matter of tact on the part of the analyst in making interpretations, and of faith in the analyst on the part of the neurotic. This suggestive influence serves not "for suppressing the symptoms—this distinguishes the analytic method from other psychotherapeutic procedures—but as a motive force to induce the patient to overcome resistances" (p. 225), a view that is still very important today. The chapter ends with the formulation handed down in psychoanalytic institutes: whoever "has passed through such a course of instruction, who has been analyzed himself, . . . [and] who has learnt the delicate technique of psycho-analysis, the art of interpretation, . . . is *no longer a layman in the field of psychoanalysis*" (p. 228; emphasis in original).

Here Freud is playing on the double meaning of the word *layman*, which he is now contrasting not with "physician" but with "scholar" or "intellectual." The chapter is a violent, formal attack on physicians, with specific reference to the American decision to associate the practice of psychoanalysis with medical training. Moreover, Freud often observed that the wish to cure—the *furor sanandi* or caretaking to the point of madness—may be an obstacle to psychoanalytic treatment itself.

THE POLITICAL STAKES

At the end of this chapter, Freud takes a position on the rules for practicing psychoanalysis. What is important, he says, is not to exclude nonphysicians but to determine the conditions under which practicing psychoanalysis will be permitted to all those who wish it, establishing some authority from whom candidates may inform themselves about what analysis is and what is legitimately required in preparation for practicing it. This passage is not very clear about the juridical implications; in fact, it seems that Freud thinks psychoanalytic societies represent this juridical authority. In other words, he remains within the private, nonregulatory framework of the practice of psychoanalysis. The final chapter continues the critique of medicine in a more epistemological mode, emphasizing the point to which medical training is of no concern to the analyst. And Freud describes an ideal academy of psychoanalysis, one that would teach depth psychology, biology, "the science of sexual life," an initiation into the clinical pictures of psychiatry, and "the history of civilization, mythology, the psychology of religion, and the science of literature" (p. 246), a program that no medical school could follow.

There is a great deal at stake in this text. At the meeting of the International Psychoanalytic Association at Innsbrück in 1927, Ernest Jones, the president, organized a panel on the practice of psychoanalysis by nonphysicians, an issue that was dividing most of the societies (see Schneider 1990). Ultimately nothing in Freud's argument leads us to conclude that he favors a legal status for psychoanalysis or the psychoanalyst; the "authority" he has in mind seems to be that of the International Psychoanalytic Association.

PSYCHOANALYSIS *FARÀ DA SE*

Up until the end, and without the least diplomacy, Freud maintained his opposition to a psychoanalysis under medical auspices. In a letter written to Schrier from London on July 5, 1938, he reaffirms his view on lay analysis (cited in Jones 1957). Freud was constantly concerned to maintain the intellectual and practical autonomy of psychoanalysis, as he observes to Jung in 1911: "Fräulein Spielrein wants to subordinate the psychological material to biological considerations; this dependency is no more acceptable than a dependency on philosophy, physiology, or brain anatomy. ΨA *farà da se*" (cited in McGuire 1988, p. 286). Here he is echoing Garibaldi on the subject of Italian unity: *Italia farà da se*, "Italy will make do on its own."

15

The Fundamental Rule: The Space of the Treatment

Freud is able to articulate and elaborate the fundamental rule (*Grundregel*) organizing the space of analytic treatment only after 1912, more than twenty years after he began to invent his method of analysis. Why did it take him so long to formulate this rule that enables us to conceptualize the end of transference love, and, beyond that, the problem of separation, the problem of the body image in connection with the problem of separation, the problem of masochism against the backdrop of the entire question of the death drive, and, finally, the theory of interpretation in analysis? There is a parallel between infantile sexual theories and psychoanalytic theories: both are responses to an urgent need to form concepts. In one of his last papers, "Analysis Terminable and Interminable" (1937a), Freud reminds us that when the analyst feels at a loss in the clinical situation, he appeals to "the witch metapsychology" (p. 243). The difference between hypnosis and psychoanalysis has to do specifically with the displacements of persons.

THE FAILURE OF DORA'S ANALYSIS

The failure of the Dora case (1905a), conducted in 1900 and published five years later, stems from the fact that Freud was not taking the transference into account: "Precisely that portion of the technical work which is most difficult never came into question with the patient; for the factor of 'transference,' which is considered at the end of each case history . . . , did not come up for discussion during the short treatment" (p. 13).

In 1900 Freud was still trying to conduct an analysis without transference, and he realizes in 1905, as he writes up the Dora case, that he had not seen the transferential role Dora assigned him. She had put him in the place of Herr K., a family friend who had given her a kiss while saying that his wife meant nothing to him, while Dora was essentially hoping to get a sense of her own body from that of Frau K., not having been able to do so from the body of her mother, a woman afflicted with "housewife's psychosis." This shows how difficult it is in certain theoretical perspectives to dissociate the analyst from his position, his intervention, his role in the transference (whether he is assigned that role or assumes it himself). It is clear that if Freud had understood that he was being placed in the position of Herr K., Dora would not have had to leave him but would have been able to tell him the story of her involvement with Herr K.

One of the pertinent aspects of the fundamental rule is its bearing on the theory of interpretation, which in turn presupposes a theory of language in general and of specific languages, as well as a theory of the psychic apparatus.

TRANSFERENCE LOVE

Before looking further at the fundamental rule, we must return to transference love as described in Freud's technical papers. As early as the *Studies on Hysteria* (Breuer and Freud 1893–1895), he offers an initial formulation that he knows is at the heart of the analytic situation: "Each time my person is implicated in this way, I can postulate the existence of a transference." And, defining transference for the first time, he adds: "The existence of a transference is that of a false relation, a false connection" (p. 302). In the same passage, he describes how a third person became confused with the doctor; the term is *zusammenfallen*, "coincide": the patient made this third person coincide with the person of the analyst.

Hence, in these early years, the transference appears to Freud to be a confusion with the third person and a wish for the two to coincide. The very nature of the transference—Freud says this a bit blindly, since he does not yet know its implications—is a passion, a drive for coinciding, becoming one, coinciding being understood as denial of separation. Now, what do we see in cases of trauma, for example, childhood trauma such as incest or rape? It is that the way to escape trauma is to annul it in an attempt to refind this coinciding. Thus we can agree with Ferenczi that there is such a thing as traumatophilia, in which the traumatized person tries to reconnect with the traumatic situation. This is precisely the way Freud defines transference love: "We have no right to dispute that the state of being in love which makes its appearance in the course of analytic treatment has the character of a 'genuine' love" (1915b, p. 168). The definition he gives in 1915 of the state of being in love thus corresponds to the passion for coinciding and the horror of separation that he had noted in *Studies on Hysteria*. When, in the analytic space, it is postulated that one unconscious can arise from two, it is clear that, according to Freud's criteria, we are dealing with a passion for coinciding and a denial of separation.

THE RAT MAN

This brings us to the fundamental rule as prophylaxis against the compulsion for coincidence. Let us note the confusion of *Einfall*, the thought that suddenly appears, comes to mind, with "association," the latter to be understood in its Jungian or Freudian acceptation if we keep to the original psychoanalytic technique as used in the case of Elisabeth von R.: the invitation on the part of the analyst for patients to associate to what he himself has brought about; for example, asking Elisabeth to stand or walk and then inquiring where her pain comes from. Here, undoubtedly, we can speak of free association, but this is not the fundamental rule in the sense that it privileges the *Einfall*.

In discussing the case of the Rat Man (1909a), we observed that the fundamental rule did not begin from the time of the second session. We shall see this in the following passage, insofar as it cannot apply in the absence of its correlate, the analyst's listening: "The next day I made him pledge himself to submit to the one and only condition of treatment—namely, to say everything that came into his head, even if it was *unpleasant* to him or seemed *unimportant* or *irrelevant* or *senseless*" (p. 159; emphasis in original). To be sure, we have here (in 1907, published in 1909) the first formulation of one of the corollaries of the fundamental rule, the one concerning the patient. But in the journal Freud kept on this case, a document entirely unique in his work, we find in connection with these first sessions some important information confirming that the correlative of the fundamental rule, the analyst's part, was missing. There is a slight inaccuracy in the account of the first session; in the case report (1909a) Freud speaks of a single condition for treatment, but in the *Journal* (session of October 2) he says that there were two.

Freud is quick to discern in the Rat Man's material an idealization of men and a strong latent homosexuality, later confirmed when the patient speaks of his nursemaid, whose first name escapes him; he recalls only her surname, which is a male given name: Fräulein Peter. In his note, Freud mentions the rapid thoughts that occurred to him during the session: Peter, forgetting of the feminine name and emphasis on the masculine, which identifies the patient as a homosexual. There follows the well known scene from the second session, in which the patient speaks of a dreadful Oriental punishment: the patient breaks off, gets up, and asks to be spared the description of the details. Freud explains that he cannot spare him in a matter over which he has no power and asks him to overcome his resistance.

Earlier the patient had spoken of a cruel captain who issued orders; Freud now asks whether impalement is involved. The patient then reluctantly and with horror gives some details of the torture in which rats enter a prisoner's anus, a homosexual element Freud had noticed from the outset. The Rat Man then returns to the question of the captain who has ordered him to reimburse the lieutenant for a package containing the pince-nez he had ordered. He continues, alternating the two scenes, the whole obsessional scenario of the course of the debt that refers back to the real debt of his father, and he complains that he always comes across men who lack understanding. As we have seen, Freud comments that he himself is not cruel, whereupon the patient addresses him as "captain."

In two sessions Freud uncovers the latent homosexuality of his patient on the sole basis of the name Peter and the constant need to refer to a male third party who can serve as a guarantor (apparently forgetting his father's weakness). Through his listening more than through his interventions, Freud perceives the overdetermined homosexual dispositions of the Rat Man—which are essentially identificatory, not object-oriented—in relation to his dead father, that is, in relation to an idealization of the authority of a male third party. Freud immediately places himself outside the transference, unable to endure the idea of a homosexual transference onto his own person, telling the patient, in effect, that he, Freud, is not the cruel captain for whom the patient takes him. In other words, when the frame of the analysis is not securely established, the analyst must resort to the theorization of the frame as an element of interpretation because he does not know what space he is in, that is, he does not know that he is in a transferential space.

THE FUNDAMENTAL RULE

Let us return to two papers that discuss the fundamental rule to see how they bear on the ending of transference love and, beyond this, on the problems of separation and body image and on the theorization of the psychic apparatus, all of these involved in the termination of an analysis.

The first of these papers is entitled "Recommendations [*Ratschläge*] to Physicians Practicing Psycho-Analysis" (1912b). *Ratschläge* should be translated as "advice" in the sense of prescription, and not as "suggestions," which connotes an orientation, a course of behavior to be followed, something on the order of hypnosis. Prescription refers not to the content but to a mode of functioning, an empty frame. It marks the possibility of the analytic space, a space of uttering without utterance because it is purely formal, without content.

This paper focuses on the analyst's role in the fundamental rule. It is supplemented by "On Beginning the Treatment" (1913b), where Freud speaks of the analyst's evenly-suspended attention, like the beam of a scale in equipoise. The analyst works without a guideline. This technique "consists simply in not directing one's notice to anything in particular" (p. 111). Freud takes the time he needs in order not to place undue emphasis on any one element. In an important formula, but one that is never referred to, he asks how the analyst should proceed: "The correct behavior for an analyst lies in swinging over according to need from the one mental attitude [*psychische Einstellung,* 'psychic position'] to the other, . . . avoiding speculation" (p. 114). *Einstellung* comes from *Stelle,* place, a word Freud used of the impossible place of son and male friend that Elisabeth von R. was assigned by her father. This is the prescriptive element. When, twenty years later, Freud defines the position of the analyst, in accordance with the needs of the patient, as relocating himself from one psychic place to another, he is inspired by the way Elisabeth's father assigns her the place of son and male friend. As Freud states in "On Beginning the Treatment," the analyst is displaced in the transference: "[E]verything connected with the present situation represents a transference to the doctor, which proves suitable to serve as a first resistance" (p. 138).

Discovering the transference means discerning the place in which the analyst is put. The patient, for his part, must behave like a traveler who, sitting next to the window in his railway compartment, describes to someone sitting behind him the countryside as it passes before his gaze. There is no question whatsoever of associative activity but instead of passively letting thoughts emerge and representations occur to him.

ONE SPACE FOR TWO PSYCHES

"On Beginning the Treatment" makes a distinction that helps us to determine the theory of the psyche that corresponds to the fundamental rule: as we have seen, in the early days of psychoanalytic technique no distinction was made between what the analyst knew and what the patient knew. "It was a severe disappointment when the expected success [of lightning diagnoses] was not forthcoming. How could it be that the patient, who now knew about his traumatic experience, nevertheless still behaved as if he knew no more about it than before?" (p. 141). He gives the example of a mother who had surprised her daughter in a homosexual incident that the girl, then a prepubertal child, no longer remembered. Each time Freud mentioned this long-ago scene, the girl reacted with an attack of hysteria and the story would once again be forgotten. The girl eventually simulated imbecility and total amnesia in order to defend herself against what Freud was saying, and Freud had to acknowledge that awareness, as such, was less important than he had previously believed; the emphasis had to be placed instead on the resistances from which the patient's ignorance stemmed.

With his new insight into knowledge imposed from without and the intellectualizing position that presupposes no distinction between our own thoughts and those of another person, Freud takes into account the fact that, in analysis, there is one space for two psyches. Hence the analyst cannot act as though there were a shared knowledge or a shared language. It is on this basis—two separate sets of psychic apparatus and two different languages—that the process can operate.

The fundamental rule also sheds light on the nature and position of the analyst in a way that is very well described by François Perrier (1994) in a passage that refers to the relation of the analyst to the schizophrenic but has a wider validity:

> In order to understand schizophrenics, one must be a hysteric. In order to say anything valid about schizophrenics, one has to identify hysterically with their negativity; thus this is a message that can be formulated only at the moment when one fades away, the moment one forgets oneself, renounces oneself, to become the herald of the message of a subject who thinks of himself as a person in the negative sense of the term. [p. 297]

This is surely one of the keys to analytic functioning, this ability to "be someone and no one," to become an exile from oneself at the moment of fading away, self-forgetfulness, and self-renunciation. The definition of the fundamental rule determines the positions of the analyst and, as a result, the problem and status of analytic interpretation.

16

The Extraterritorial Space of Uttering

To conclude this survey of the work of Freud, situated in the development of his own discoveries, let us try to see how Freud would answer the following question: Can there be a psychoanalysis without ethics?

ETHICS AND METAPHYSICS

The debate about whether there can be an ethics in a separate form, that is, distinct from a religion or a world view (*Weltanschauung*) is far from a new one. With Kant (1781) we can answer yes; everything that is possible through freedom is practical, and here ethics is the ability to bring into existence a transcendental freedom, that is, a causality of reason in the determination of a will not pathologically affected by the order of phenomena governed by the causality of nature and science, at the same time that such a will is detached from a world view. With Hegel, on the other hand, we would have to say no; there is no morality in a separate form because, in *The Phenomenology of Mind* (1807), consciousness successively takes on all the modalities and phases of culture. Consciousness is thus immersed in a "crafty" reason that ultimately coincides with absolute knowledge; it never emerges from the cultural elements with which it is united. Thus to a certain extent Hegel announced that, when it coincides with wisdom (metaphysics coinciding with ethics), absolute knowledge brings us to the end of history.

We could also go through Greek philosophy and the work of other writers to demonstrate that there are well grounded positions for and against the notion that ethics exists apart from a world view. This debate on the exteriority of ethics with regard to metaphysics can direct us to the Greeks and the fact that, in antiquity, there was no freedom. The concept of freedom—autonomy from the order of nature and the cosmos—that came with the Kantian revolution does not exist before that. The subject is a microcosm, that is, a fragment of the cosmos, a parcel of divine intelligence and not separate from it. In the Greek world, morality can only be assent to the order of the world, following what is appropriate, customary. Thus there are, on the one hand, *ta kathekonta*, the things that are appropriate, and, on the other hand, *ta ou kathekonta*, the things that are not appropriate. Morality is thus reduced to *ethos*, custom. Freud states that this world of coherence between metaphysics, ethics, and religion has ended for modern man, and he offers his own mythology. What he is aiming at, and the stakes he is trying to uphold, is the autonomy of analytic practice both from a world view and from ethics.

CULT OF THE FATHER, CULT OF THE DEAD

Before turning to Freud's mythology—*Totem and Taboo* (1913a) and *Moses and Monotheism* (1939a)—since the purpose of doing so is to show that the Freudian revolution marks the end of patriarchy, the end of the debt owed to the father, we must consider the cult of the dead in classical civilizations. In traditional societies and classical antiquity, "father" (*pater*) is not a term relating to personal fatherhood. Benveniste (1969, pp. 209–215) notes that *pater*, in all of the Indo-European languages, never refers to physical paternity associated with procreation but is an attribute of God (etymologically, *Jupiter* is *diu pater*, father of the day, father of the sky, of light; the Latin *dies* refers to the *diu* in his name). This suggests that the father is derived from the figure of God. In archaic Latin, the father is *atta*, the personal father, the nurturer, the father who raises the child. This explains the Latin saying *pater est quem nuptiae demonstrant*: the father is not the progenitor but the one who is attested, demonstrated, by the wedding. Before he is a biological father, he is the mother's husband.

Classical culture thus privileges the *zoë*, the living, over the *bios*, biological life. Already we can see here a kind of affirmation of the symbolic victory of vitality over vitalism, impersonal life, desacralized life (to which we are returning today with biotechnology). At the same time, the father has an essential, sacerdotal function in the cult of the dead. Indeed, the fathers who organize the life of the city, and one spoke not of the citizenry but of the fathers, the elders, each of whom brought offerings to the shades of the dead at the ancestral altar of his family. We can thus state (and this is equally true of Chinese society, which is also devoted to the cult of the dead) that the father's function is to make sure that the ancestor is not condemned to starvation.

The dead father, insofar as he is celebrated in the ancestor, owes his survival to the living. And here there is a reversal, since the ancestor is weak and simultaneously weakens the father, who is merely at the service of the dead. The father–ancestor is weak because, in his devouring orality that asks the living for more and more life and refuses to die, he is dependent on the living to fulfill his imperious and urgent demand. This is the meaning of the legal adage to the effect that the dead take hold of the living: the ancestor engulfs, vampirizes the living. From this perspective, patricide on the part of the son is not killing the father but no longer feeding the ancestor.

FREUDIAN MYTHOLOGY

Freud arranges things differently. In this context, "mythology" does not have the pejorative connotation of naiveté; it is a world view that assures man a place in the universe. Hobbes' *Leviathan* (1651) is a "mythology" in this sense, a political myth. Likewise, when Jean-Jacques Rousseau wrote his *Discourse on the Origin of Inequality* (1755), he constructed a "mythology"; paragraph 6 begins with an exhortation to discard all facts on the grounds of their irrelevance.

Lévi-Strauss objects to Freud's theory of totemism, but Freud was not aiming at a historical view of origins. He was creating a "mythology" in which the father had to be put to death so that the living could live. Let us turn

to Freud's first Moses, an article that appeared anonymously in *Imago* in 1914 (and not until 1924 under
Freud's own name). "The Moses of Michelangelo" (1914d)
is just as contrary to historical truth as the Moses book
written at the end of Freud's life. What fascinates Freud,
who often went to San Pietro ai Vincoli when he visited
Rome to see the Moses destined for the tomb of Pope
Julius II, is the lack of restraint in this head, its anger.
Freud wonders whether Moses is going to break the tab-
lets of the Law in reaction to a people who sacrificed the
golden calf, or whether he has another position, not that
of the all-powerful *Urvater*.

This short paper is the account of a fantasy of Freud's,
in which he sees in this Moses someone holding back from
acting (*agieren*), getting control of his anger. The German
word for "act" also means "crime," and this Moses stops
the crime against the son, the infanticide and the cult of
the dead that had kept calling for the sons' blood. Moses'
becoming an Egyptian means the killing of the great man,
which we find in a different modality in *Totem and Taboo*,
the patricide said to occur as the founding act of culture,
the murder of the father necessary to set a limit to his in-
finite enjoyment as possessor of all the women. This murder, therefore, is not to be understood in a chronological
sense. It is not placed at a historical starting point but is
a myth of origin marking the conditions of possibility for
later existence. Likewise the Book of Genesis in the Bible
is not a history book but a book of origins about the conditions of possibility of human history, a history that can
exist only in finitude, that is, outside the earthly paradise

in which the self is fully realized to itself and in the encounter with the other.

EMERGENCE OF THE LAW

The murder of the father is the first requirement for the pact of the brothers, since it makes it impossible for omnipotence ever again to arise in reality, and it occurs in order to mark a law founding the prohibition of incest and the restriction of the drives (*Triebeinschränkung*), which is ethics. There is a logical continuity between *Totem and Taboo* and *Moses and Monotheism*. The emergence of the Law that undoes the omnipotence of the *Urvater* simultaneously puts an end to the state of indebtedness to ancestors and permits time to open out toward the future, that is, to a posterity. The Freudian gesture thus reverses the position of classical culture.

In *The Interpretation of Dreams* (1900) Freud recounts the so-called "dream of the revolutionary," a dream of Count Thun, a minister of Franz Josef, who was nicknamed "inaction" because of his inefficiency, "Thun" being a homonym of *Tun*, "action." In the dream, Freud sees him in his carriage and thinks that he would rather be an ancestor. This symbolically marks *The Interpretation of Dreams*, whose seventh chapter, dealing with the question of a historical beginning that does not refer to the *Urvater*, was written after the death of Freud's father.

When Freud says that he would rather be an ancestor, he is responding to Chateaubriand (1844) who had written, in connection with the decadence of the aristocracy, that people count their ancestors when they no longer count. Here we are, then, in the Freudian revolution, with a guilt that completely changes its meaning from the notion that we must not separate ourselves from our ancestors to the words beginning Chapter 7 of *Civilisation and Its Discontents* (1930).

CULTURE AND REPRESSION OF THE DRIVES

But before looking at this chapter, we must go back to a paper that is sometimes considered Reichian, "'Civilised' Sexual Morality and Modern Nervous Illness" (1908b), in which Freud asks how one is to locate oneself in culture and to what extent culture is merely in the service of suppressing the drives (a question Marcuse took up in *Eros and Civilization* [1968], where he confuses suppression and repression). Freud states that

> Each individual has surrendered some part of his possessions—some part of the sense of omnipotence or of the aggressive or vindictive inclinations in his personality. . . . Besides the exigencies of life . . . [t]he man who, in consequence of his unyielding constitution, cannot fall in with the suppression of instinct becomes a 'criminal,' an 'outlaw,' in the face of society—unless his social position or his exceptional capacities enable him to impose himself upon it as a great man, a hero. [pp. 186–187]

When Freud returns in 1939 to "the great man" in his study of Moses and monotheistic religion, the models of his "great men" will be Goethe, Leonardo da Vinci, and Beethoven, those who favor the restriction of drives and have a high aptitude for sublimation. The nostalgia for the father, the cult of the father to which Freud puts an end in what was to be called his "mythology," is revealed in *Moses and Monotheism*: "We know that, in the mass of humanity, there exists the strong need for an authority whom we can admire, before whom we bow down, by whom we are dominated and possibly even mistreated; individual psychology has taught us where this need for the group comes from. It is nostalgia for the father" (p. 101).

THE SENSE OF GUILT

This text introduces us to Chapter 7 of *Civilisation and Its Discontents*, where Freud describes the secret of guilt, the feeling of debt with regard to the origin (to use an expression of Nietzsche's in *The Genealogy of Morals* [1887]): that unpayable debt that may cause one to become a criminal. The criminal may be so subjected to morality that he can never acquit the debt and free himself of it, the only way of escaping it being to commit a crime to prove that he is, finally, guilty in reality and not only in his fantasies (cf. "The criminal from a sense of guilt" in Freud 1916, where Nietzsche is cited). Guilt is defined as the inability to separate from an external object. For Freud, it is the impossibility of ending a permanent and indissoluble bond with one of the modalities of culture, for example religion or metaphysics. It implies the existence of a prosthetic ego that can exist only in a dependent union with the external object (which, clearly, may be an ideal object), whereas in classical culture guilt arose from the failure to look after one's father or mother, from not being in a permanent sacrificial relation to him or her. Here Freud demonstrates that guilt stems from not daring to separate from this father, and the present malaise in culture, as he sees it, has to do with human beings' horror of separation and individuation. Thus his mythology confirms the end of the classical world, the end of a system of representations to which human beings were subjected, and the logical correlate, the destruction of the cult of the ancestor and the patriarchy formed in the image of God.

THE DISENCHANTMENT OF THE WORLD

In other words, Freud's opening move can be said to be: there is no correspondence between the cosmos and the individual. Here he is in the tradition of those who, as Max Weber put it, are beginning the disenchantment of the world, those who take divinity out of the world, driving away the gods of Greece who were present in the universe at a time when one of the most beautiful celebrations was Hölderlin's "Hyperion" (1797), which describes this experience of total plenitude, total reconciliation of man with man and man with nature. It is Hölderlin who, in his madness for real presence, *parousia*, went the furthest in his fascination with this harmony in which there is no longer a gap in human life. Yet this is the same Hölderlin who, at the end of his life, ended a poem entitled "The Vocation of the Poet" with the affirmation that, if necessary, man can stand before God without fear; protected by his candor, he has no need of arms or trickery until the time when only the absence of God can come to his aid.

FREUDIAN METAPSYCHOLOGY

This brings us to a Freudian metapsychology that is no longer bound up with a world view or a metaphysics. Here we must recall that crucial passage, rarely mentioned in the psychoanalytic literature, from the third part of "On Beginning the Treatment" (1913b), in which, as we have seen, Freud speaks of distinguishing between what the patient knows and what the analyst knows. In other words, he had to leave an intellectualizing position behind in order to realize that there is no unconscious shared by analyst and patient and that the Freudian subject has a separate body, psyche, and knowledge. The analyst is absolutely ignorant of what is going on in the patient's head, and here Freud notes that, when he was not distinguishing what he knew from what the patient knew, he would fill the patient with alien knowledge, imposed from without. This type of intellectualizing psychoanalysis amounted to a hypnotic therapy and a brainwashing of the patient. To paraphrase the famous "Where It was, I should come into being," we might say "where the patient's It [id] was, the analyst's I [ego] should come into being." We have to keep in mind this radical disjunction between mythology and metapsychology if we are to leave this universe in which analyst and analysand have a conjoined awareness.

THE SPACE OF UTTERING

The result for psychoanalytic technique was a total reversal, since, up to then, it was the analyst who hypnotized the patient, filling him with his knowledge, whereas the technical analytic position is to enable the analysand to find a space of uttering. Freud describes this reversal, in which the patient "hypnotizes" the analyst, in "Recommendations to Physicians Practicing Psycho-Analysis" (1912b), the inverse of what he had said earlier about the analyst being in an *intellektualistischer Denkeinstellung*, a position of intellectualized thinking; here the analyst must adopt a *psychische Einstellung*, a psychic position, according to the needs of the patient. In Freud's view, the analytic relation is based on a psychic temporality (one that has nothing to do with the Greenwich meridian governing our vectorized sense of time), in which the analyst must be in synchrony with the other's unconscious and syntonic with his affects. The passage to the psychic position, the analysand's psychic summons to the analyst, reverses what happens in ordinary life. The analysis is the place where a patient can free himself from subjection to prescriptive speech that has put him in impossible situations (as when Elisabeth von R. heard her father tell her that she was his son and male friend), reproducing that prescriptive violence on the analyst so that he can withdraw from these original deadly assignments.

ETHICS AND METHOD

If every ethics today is the recognition of alterity, it could be said that the analytic relation is not absolutely governed by an ethics, since it presupposes the negation of all the analyst's unique characteristics, the analyst being present not *in propria persona* but in place of an other who is missing or lacking in the patient's life. Thus psychoanalysis does not have a relational ethics in the sense that it is not possible and viable for someone except in this "house arrest" of the analyst in a place required by the patient. But this is the condition of acquitting one's debts to one's creator. In other words, psychoanalysis is more a method—a unique method of speaking—than an ethics. Psychoanalysis marks the end of guilt, settling accounts and thereby opening out into respect for the other instead of resentment and an ongoing debt to one's ancestors and to great men. It is not the transmission of a system of representation, but it enables us, in each individual case, to examine the ways in which a subject has encountered history—cultural history, family history—and how he has been able to change these histories a little. Change them, or reevaluate them in that extraterritorial space of uttering that is an analytic treatment.

References

Benveniste, E. (1969). *Le Vocabulaire des institutions européens*, vol. 1 Paris: Minuit.

Breuer, J., and Freud, S. (1893–1895). *Studies on Hysteria. Standard Edition* 2.

Chateaubriand, F. R. (1844). *La Vie de l'abbé de Rancé*. Paris: Minuit, 1981.

Freud, E. L., ed. (1960). *Letters of Sigmund Freud*. New York: Dover.

Freud, S. (1887–1902). *The Origins of Psychoanalysis. Letters to Wilhelm Fliess, Drafts, and Notes*, ed. M. Bonaparte, A. Freud, and E. Kris, trans. E. Mosbacher and J. Strachey. New York: Basic Books, 1954.

——— (1894). The neuro-psychoses of defence. *Standard Edition* 3:41–61.

——— (1895). Project for a scientific psychology. *Standard Edition* 1:281–397.

——— (1900). *The Interpretation of Dreams. Standard Edition* 4–5.

——— (1901a). *The Psychopathology of Everyday Life. Standard Edition* 6.

——— (1901b). *On Dreams. Standard Edition* 5:629–686.

—— (1905a). Fragment of an analysis of a case of hysteria. *Standard Edition* 7:1–122.

—— (1905b). *Jokes and Their Relation to the Unconscious. Standard Edition* 8.

—— (1905c). *Three Essays on the Theory of Sexuality. Standard Edition* 7:123–243.

—— (1905d). Psychical (or mental) treatment. *Standard Edition* 7:281–302.

—— (1907). *Delusions and Dreams in Jensen's "Gradiva." Standard Edition* 9:1–95.

—— (1908a). On the sexual theories of children. *Standard Edition* 9:205–226.

—— (1908b). "Civilised" sexual morality and modern nervous illness. *Standard Edition* 9:177–204.

—— (1909a). Notes upon a case of obsessional neurosis. *Standard Edition* 10:151–249.

—— (1909b). Analysis of a phobia in a five-year-old boy. *Standard Edition* 10:1–147.

—— (1909c). Original record of the case. *Standard Edition* 10:251–318.

—— (1909d). De la genèse du fétichisme. In *Revue internationale d'histoire de la psychanalyse* 2:423–439, 1989.

—— (1910a). *Five Lectures on Psycho-Analysis. Standard Edition* 11:1–55.

—— (1910b). *Leonardo da Vinci and a Memory of His Childhood. Standard Edition* 11:57–137.

—— (1910c). "Wild" psycho-analysis. *Standard Edition* 11:219–227.

—— (1911a). Psycho-analytic notes on an autobiographical account of a case of paranoia (dementia paranoides). *Standard Edition* 12:1–79.

—— (1911b). The handling of dream-interpretation in psychoanalysis. *Standard Edition* 12:89–96.

——— (1911c). Formulations on the two principles of mental functioning. *Standard Edition* 12:213–226.

——— (1912a). The dynamics of transference. *Standard Edition* 12:97–108.

——— (1912b). Recommendations to physicians practicing psycho-analysis. *Standard Edition* 12:109–120.

——— (1913a). *Totem and Taboo. Standard Edition* 13:1–161.

——— (1913b). On beginning the treatment. *Standard Edition* 12:121–144.

——— (1913c). The claims of psycho-analysis to scientific interest. *Standard Edition* 13:163–190.

——— (1913d). The theme of the three caskets. *Standard Edition* 12:289–301.

——— (1914a). On narcissism: an introduction. *Standard Edition* 14:67–102.

——— (1914b). On the history of the psycho-analytic movement. *Standard Edition* 14:1–66.

——— (1914c). Remembering, repeating and working-through. *Standard Edition* 12:145–156.

——— (1914d). The Moses of Michelangelo. *Standard Edition* 13:209–236.

——— (1915a). The unconscious. *Standard Edition* 14:159–215.

——— (1915b). Observations on transference love. *Standard Edition* 12:157–171.

——— (1915c). Repression. *Standard Edition* 14:141–158.

——— (1916). Some character-types met with in psycho-analytic work. *Standard Edition* 14:309–335.

——— (1917a). *Introductory Lectures on Psycho-Analysis. Standard Edition* 15–16.

——— (1917b). Mourning and melancholia. *Standard Edition* 14:237–259.

——— (1918). From the history of an infantile neurosis. *Standard Edition* 17:1–122.

—— (1919a). Lines of advance in psycho-analytic therapy. *Standard Edition* 17:157–168.

—— (1919b). "A child is being beaten." *Standard Edition* 17:175–204.

—— (1919c). The "uncanny." *Standard Edition* 17:217–256.

—— (1920). *Beyond the Pleasure Principle. Standard Edition* 18:1–64.

—— (1921). *Group Psychology and the Analysis of the Ego. Standard Edition* 18:65–143.

—— (1922). Remarks on the theory and practice of dream-interpretation. *Standard Edition* 19:107–121.

—— (1923a). Psycho-analysis. *Standard Edition* 20:259–270.

—— (1923b). Libido theory. *Standard Edition* 23:235–259.

—— (1923c). *The Ego and the Id. Standard Edition* 19:1–59.

—— (1924a). Neurosis and psychosis. *Standard Edition* 19:147–153.

—— (1924b). The economical problem of masochism. *Standard Edition* 19:155–170.

—— (1924c). The dissolution of the Oedipus complex. *Standard Edition* 19:171–179.

—— (1925a). *An Autobiographical Study. Standard Edition* 19:171–179.

—— (1925b). The resistances to psycho-analysis. *Standard Edition* 20:1–70.

—— (1925c). Negation. *Standard Edition* 19:233–239.

—— (1926a). *Inhibitions, Symptoms and Anxiety. Standard Edition* 20:75–174.

—— (1926b). *The Question of Lay Analysis. Standard Edition* 20:177–250.

—— (1927a). *The Future of an Illusion. Standard Edition* 21:1–56.

—— (1927b). Fetishism. *Standard Edition* 21:147–157.

—— (1928). Dostoyevsky and patricide. *Standard Edition* 21:173–194

—— (1930). *Civilisation and Its Discontents. Standard Edition* 21:57–145.

—— (1931). Female sexuality. *Standard Edition* 21:221–243.

—— (1932a). The acquisition and control of fire. *Standard Edition* 22:183–193.

—— (1932b). Why war? *Standard Edition* 22:195–215.

—— (1933). *New Introductory Lectures on Psycho-Analysis. Standard Edition* 22:1–182.

—— (1936). A disturbance of memory on the Acropolis. *Standard Edition* 22:237–248.

—— (1937a). Analysis terminable and interminable. *Standard Edition* 23:209–253.

—— (1937b). Constructions in analysis. *Standard Edition* 23:255–269.

—— (1939a). *Moses and Monotheism. Standard Edition* 23:1–137.

—— (1939b). Splitting of the ego in the process of defence. *Standard Edition* 23:271–278.

—— (1939c). *An Outline of Psycho-Analysis. Standard Edition* 23:139–207.

Grubrich-Simitis, I. (1997). *Freud: Retour aux manuscrits*. Paris: PUF.

Hegel, G. F. (1807). *The Phenomenology of Mind*, trans. J. B. Baillie. New York: Dover, 1987.

Hobbes, T. (1651). *Leviathan*. New York: Penguin, 1982.

Hölderlin, F. (1797). *Hyperion and Selected Poems*, trans. M. Hamburger. New York: Continuum, 1982.

Jones, E. (1955). *The Life and Work of Sigmund Freud. Vol. 2: The Years of Maturity, 1901–1919*. New York: Basic Books.

—— (1957). *The Life and Work of Sigmund Freud. Vol. 3: The Last Phase, 1919–1939*. New York: Basic Books.

Jung, C. G. (1912). Transformations and symbols of the libido. In *The Collected Works of C. G. Jung*, ed. H. Read, M. Fordham, and G. Adler, trans. R. F. C. Hull, Vol. 5: *Symbols of Transformation*, pp. 26–55. Princeton, NJ: Princeton University Press, 1952.

Kant, I. (1781). *Critique of Pure Reason*, trans. N. K. Smith. New York: Macmillan, 2003.

Lacan, J. (1964). *Séminaire XI*. Paris: Seuil, 1973.

——— (1977). *Ecrits. A Selection*, trans. A. Sheridan. New York: Norton.

Laplanche, J., and Pontalis, J.-B. (1973). *The Language of Psycho-Analysis*. London: Hogarth.

Lawrence, T. E. (1922). *The Mint*. London: Cape, 1955.

Le Bon, G. (1896). *Psychologie du socialisme*. Paris: Les Amis de G. Le Bon, 1977.

Mannoni, O. (1969). *Clefs pour l'imaginaire*. Paris: Seuil.

Marcuse, H. (1968). *Eros and Civilization*. New York: Beacon, 1974.

McDougall, W. (1920). *The Group Mind*. New York: Putnam.

McGuire, W., ed. (1988). *The Freud/Jung Letters. The Correspondence Between Sigmund Freud and Carl Gustav Jung*, trans. R. Manheim and R. F. C. Hull. Cambridge, MA: Harvard University Press.

Moscovici, S. (1981). *L'Âge des foules*. Paris: Fayard.

Nietzsche, F. (1887). *Genealogy of Morals*, trans. W. Kaufmann. New York: Vintage, 1988.

Nunberg, H., and Federn, E., eds. (1962–1975). *Minutes of the Vienna Psychoanalytic Society*, vol 2, trans. M. Nunberg and H. Collins. New York: International Universities Press.

Perrier, F. (1994). *La Chaussée d'Antin*. Paris: Albin Michel.

Pontalis, J.-B. (1985). Introduction to Freud's *Die Frage der Laienanalyse*. Paris: Gallimard.

Rousseau, J.-J. (1755). *Discourse on the Origin of Inequality*, trans. D. A. Cress. New York: Hackett, 1992.

Schneider, M. (1990). La "Question" en débat. *Revue internationale d'histoire de la psychanalyse* 3.

Trotter, W. (1916). *Instincts of the Herd in Peace and War*. New York: Macmillan.

Index